CHRISTIANITY AND REAL LIFE

WILLIAM E. DIEHL

FORTRESS PRESS   Philadelphia

CONTENTS

To all those dear friends in our various Christian support groups who helped enrich my pilgrimage of faith—our first group in Detroit, and then the Face-to-Face group of Devon, the FOCUS Community and Channel 2 of Allentown, and the K Group of Emmaus in Pennsylvania—and with thanks to that lifelong support group of Judy, Shelley and Gordon, Bill and Beth, Buffy, and Jennifer.

PREFACE

This book is about two gaps.

The first gap is the one which is present in my life and in the lives of thousands of dedicated Christian laypeople. It is the gap between our Sunday faith and our weekday world.

The second gap is the one which is present in the life of the institutional church. It is the gap between what the church proclaims as the role of Christian laypersons in the world and what the church actually does to support that role.

The two gaps are clearly interrelated.

As long as I can remember, my church has been proclaiming that all believers are called to be ministers. Although we have ordained clergy, my church says that there is a priesthood of all believers. My church operates on the theory that if the congregation of believers comes together for worship, study, and fellowship, then the laity will go into the world to minister to others with the love and acceptance which God has given to them. My church has been telling me that I am to be a "little Christ" to others with whom I come in contact. That's what my church has been *saying*.

What has my church been *doing* to support my ministry in the various arenas of my life? Very little.

I am now a sales manager for a major steel company. In the almost thirty years of my professional career, my church has never once suggested that there be any type of accounting of my on-the-job ministry to others. My church has never once offered to improve those skills which could make me a better minister, nor has it ever asked if I needed any kind of support in what I was doing. There has never been an inquiry into the types of ethical decisions I must face, or whether I seek to communicate the faith to my co-workers. I have never been in a congregation where there was any type of public affirmation of a ministry in my career. In short, I must conclude that my church really doesn't have the least interest in whether or how I minister in my daily work.

Judy and I were married in the church, our four children were baptized in the church, and together we have participated in the total life of a number of different congregations. The church consistently called us to worship and service in its corporate structure, but provided virtually no support for our ministries to members of our family. We have never been confronted with an accounting of our ministries to those other family members who were not associated with our congregation, such as elderly parents or troubled brothers or sisters. When our older children left home for college and marriage, it was—so far as my parish was concerned—as if they had left the face of the earth. I have concluded that my church cares only about my ministry to those members of my family who are also a part of that congregation; it really doesn't care about my ministry to the others.

The dimension of my life which involves community concerns has been varied and sometimes stormy. Over the years we have been involved in the civil rights movement and the peace movement; we have worked with kids on probation and with ex-offenders, tried to improve local government, and sought to be advocates for the poor and powerless of our society. These activities were a direct response to the teachings of my faith. And yet my church gave no evidence of really supporting my ministries in the community outside the walls of our congregation. On the contrary, there were times when I was made to feel guilty because a commitment to community ministry interfered with a request for service within the congregation.

I am not alone in my disillusionment. On the basis of personal conversations as well as surveys conducted by the churches themselves it is obvious to me that many other laypeople too feel that the church has all but abandoned them in their weekday world.

How can I reconcile this disillusionment with the fact that I also give large chunks of my time in service to the church? For almost thirty years I have served in various capacities in our congregational, regional, and national committees and agencies. I am presently on the Executive Council of the Lutheran Church in America.

There was a time in my life when I had completely rejected religion and was not connected with any church. But certain traumatic events caused me to reconsider my position. As a combat medic with a tank batallion in Europe during the Second World War, I helped to pull screaming men from burning tanks, administered first aid to my best friend whose leg was blown off, saw men die, and spent many nights shivering with fear. As the war drew to a close and we began to liberate prisons and concentration camps, I was brought face to face with that unspeakable brutality of our human existence, the Holocaust in which six million Jews were murdered.

These events caused me to reexamine my faith and the meaning of life itself. I began a pilgrimage of faith which has also involved active roles in that historic channel of the faith, the church.

But if one takes seriously the claims of the Christian faith, one must also be troubled by the question of integrity within the institutional church. If there is a gap between what we say and what we do, we will either be caught in the hypocrisy or we will become indifferent.

When my church preaches about the ministry of the laity, it speaks in broad and idealistic terms; but when it comes down to reality, my church sees lay ministry purely in terms of service to the institutional church. My church proclaims the ministry of laypersons in the world; it practices the encouragement of lay ministries solely within the church—in teaching, leading worship, visiting members, serving on local, regional, and national committees, and giving time and money to the organization.

I believe this gap is not intentional. Furthermore, I believe it can be bridged.

This book will explore the present institutional schizophrenia of lay ministry. It will explain why the church is caught in a box and what can be done to get out of it. It will also explore a number of possibilities for vital lay ministry in the world today, and how they can be developed.

As a layman I believe in lay ministry. I believe too that the freeing up of Christian laypeople for ministries in our society is needed for the welfare of humanity, for the integrity of our Christian faith, and for the very survival of the church as an institution.

1.

SOMETHING
IS
MISSING

In February 1975, the chairman of the board of a large multinational corporation jumped to his death from the forty-fourth floor of the Pan-Am Building in Manhattan. Many of the eastern newspapers reported the suicide, but it was the *Wall Street Journal* which searched beyond the superficial facts. In a feature article on its front page, the *Journal* reviewed the life of Eli M. Black and asked a penetrating question: "Can a sensitive man, a man with high moral standards, survive in an uncompromising financial world that demands steadily increasing earnings?"

Eli Black was a religious man. He was graduated from Yeshiva University in 1940 and served as rabbi of a congregation on Long Island for four years. Because he felt unfulfilled as a rabbi, he decided to carry his concerns for people into a business profession. After a number of years of highly successful performance in several different companies, he found himself chairman of United Brands Company, formerly known as United Fruit Company. His social concerns remained a large part of his purpose in life.

"When he acquired United Fruit," reported the *Wall Street Journal*, "he was as equally dedicated to achieving earnings growth as he was to obliterating the old United Fruit image of being a Yankee exploiter." In Honduras and elsewhere, Eli Black's companies supplied benefits to the workers far beyond those granted by similar multinationals. In 1972 the *Boston Globe* reported that United Brands "may well be the most socially conscious American company in the hemisphere." Eli Black negotiated personally with Cesar Chavez's United Farm Workers Union and became the first and only major lettuce grower to sign with the union.

But 1974 was a disaster-plagued year for United Brands, and although the worst seemed to be behind him, by February the strain had been overwhelming. After a short period of depression Eli Black leaped to his death.

In the weeks and months following his suicide the American people were able to learn of the overwhelming pressures which had come to bear on Mr. Black. First there was the revelation that United Brands had secretly made a $1.25 million payoff to a Honduras official to reduce that country's banana tax. Newspaper articles speculated over whether or not Mr. Black was aware of the bribe and if the discovery of it played a part in his decision to take his own life.

Next came stories of tremendous power struggles within the board of United Brands including efforts of some executives to seize control of the corporation. Given the fact that this chief executive of a large multinational corporation was trying to integrate a social conscience into his organization at a time when it was facing financial disaster, was involved in secret payoffs, and was being rocked by an inner power struggle, one can well imagine the kinds of pressure which beset this sensitive man.

The *Wall Street Journal* summed it up well: "A rabbi by training, a businessman by inclination, he believed that he could straddle the two worlds successfully by combining business with a social conscience and sensitivity. In the end, the pressure from two worlds split him apart."

What about the Eli Blacks of our society? Where do they get their encouragement and support? There usually is a staff of business associates who will provide support for the wrenching business decisions which have to be made. But from what direction comes the personal support when an Eli Black tries to stimulate the social conscience of his organization? Does his religious community offer support? Does it care? Does it even know?

Several years ago, a friend of ours, who is a deeply religious person and has great talent for getting people to work together in small groups, decided she had to get more involved in trying to help solve some of the problems facing the poor in our city. Nancy Smith joined several community groups which focused on human relations and on housing for the poor.

Because of her ability to work effectively with small groups and because of her deep commitment to the cause of social justice, Nancy soon found herself in important leadership positions in several community organizations. More and more demands were made upon her time. She began to be less active in the program of her church. At first nothing was said. But as time went on Nancy began to encounter questions and criticism from fellow church members because she wasn't active anymore. At times she actually felt guilty about not supporting her religious organizations better.

When the time came for a citizens' review of the local prison system, Nancy was selected to direct the program. The report she wrote was honest and of very high quality. Our local prison system had many shortcomings, and that had to be said. Although state correctional officials widely praised the study, many local officials were upset and critical both of the report and of Nancy. The president judge of the county and the county commissioners began speaking out in public against "that Smith woman."

But perhaps the most bitter disappointment came when Nancy began to receive criticism from some of her fellow church members. There were questions which implied that she was primarily interested in personal notoriety. There were statements which suggested that a true Christian is a peacemaker in the community, not a troublemaker. And there was a noticeable coolness which she could observe from a number of her fellow believers whenever she met them, in church or outside.

Nancy received support and encouragement from her family and other socially concerned people in the civic groups to which she belonged. Her personal hurts and struggles were shared with these people—not with her fellow church members. As she strove to relate the teachings of her faith to her personal ministry in her community she found herself totally abandoned by her church. After discussing the situation at home over a period of time, she and her family decided to leave their church. "And," sighs Nancy with a wistful smile, "nobody really cared that we left."

Several months ago I was asked to be a resource person for a group of teenagers enjoying a weekend family camping experience. The youth themselves had decided to spend four hours discussing Alvin Toffler's book, *Future Shock*, and the short movie adapted from it. I was curious as to how they had arrived at this decision. It had been years since *Future Shock* had been a best seller, so their choice couldn't have been related to its current popularity. Several days before the camping weekend I reviewed the book and marked sections for special consideration by the group.

At the appropriate time in the weekend schedule, the adults went off for a special event and I was left with about ten young people, aged twelve to sixteen. First we saw the movie and talked about it. Then we discussed portions of the book itself. We talked about how human beings react to being overstimulated by too much happening in too short a time. The young people quickly put this definition of future shock into the framework of crises they were being exposed to every day on the television news broadcasts: world hunger, war threats in the Middle East, energy shortage, inflation, scandal in government, pollution of the environment, rising crime rates, and increased drug usage in the schools.

We discussed each of these issues and, of course, there were no easy answers. But as we progressed I began to see that the four-hour agenda on *Future Shock* had really been promoted by one of the older girls, Julie. The real question in Julie's mind was how to overcome all the hopelessness and depression teenagers feel whenever they seriously consider the current problems facing our society. She was partially concerned about the problems themselves, but she was more concerned about how her friends in school were reacting to these seemingly unsolvable issues.

Julie comes from a religious family. She participates in a Christian education program at the church. Her parents are committed to a lifestyle in which the religious dimension is strong. Her father and mother care deeply about people and have effectively ministered to the needs of many people in our community. Although Julie's family is not the type that has a pat answer for all problems, they do communicate a spirit which says that life has meaning and purpose.

Julie was truly concerned about her friends at school. She said most of them were convinced that the future was hopeless. They were often depressed. They saw no purpose in life. Many of them were into drugs and various bizarre activities.

Although the world's problems frightened Julie also, she recognized that inside her there was a sense of hope, a feeling that life had meaning. She wanted to communicate this feeling to her friends because she really cared about them. But her religious pilgrimage had not yet progressed to the point where she could either articulate or communicate her inner feelings. In short, Julie felt a calling to minister to her friends at school but didn't have the faintest idea of how to express herself.

I asked her if she had ever discussed her concerns at Sunday church school. She said no. When I encouraged her to do so she said, "Well, we really don't have time for that kind of thing."

No time for Julie's ministry? At an age in her life when she's beginning to break the ties with home and establish her own individuality, where does Julie go for support in her efforts to help her friends if her church program doesn't have time for Julie's agenda?

Chris Wayne is a physician. I first met Chris many years ago when we were team-teaching a group of high school students in a Christian education program in our church. At that time, Chris was doing some exciting research work involving the nervous system at a prominent medical school, as well as teaching medical students.

Chris and I worked hard at trying to present the teachings of our faith to these young people in a way which really related to their lives. As we met with each other to plan lessons, the conversation often drifted toward our own personal struggles to relate our faith to our daily life. Chris was struggling with his own career. Although he could see that he was serving society in medical research and teaching, he felt that his calling as a physician was not truly being fulfilled unless he was dealing directly with the sick and injured. He was particularly distressed about the inadequate medical treatment available to the poor people in the slums of our big cities.

"It's just awful," he would say. "If you or I get hit by a car in downtown Philadelphia we get taken to a hospital and our family doctor is immediately notified. He sees to it that we get the benefit of the proper specialists and he takes a direct interest in our welfare. But when someone from the ghetto is admitted to a hospital," he continued, "he is treated by an intern who is assigned for duty at that time. The interns are young, inexperienced, and really more interested in completing their own training program than in taking a deep interest in the patients. Poor people are problems to be disposed of. So the interns slap a band-aid on them and put them out on the streets again."

Each time we talked I could see that Chris was moving more and more toward a career change. His inclinations were totally related to his faith. He felt that as a doctor, and a Christian, he had to be ministering to people directly. We talked about Luther's teaching that a Christian can serve God in almost any field of work. Surely medical research was important, I pointed out. We talked about Jesus. Chris saw Jesus as a teacher and a healer, but not as a researcher. Chris clearly saw a Christian ministry for himself in the emergency room of a big city hospital; he did not see it as clearly in the research labs of an Ivy League medical school.

For Chris to proceed in the direction his faith was taking him would be to impose a great sacrifice upon his family. He discovered that hospitals would be glad to hire him, but their budgets were such that they could pay him no more than that which an intern earns. With four children approaching college age, that represented an incredible financial strain for him. Furthermore, emergency room duty was not nine to five on weekdays only. Like the interns he would have to take his turn at nighttime and weekend duty. That meant less time with his family, and he saw his responsibilities there too.

Because his career struggle so clearly was related to his faith, it seemed to me that the church might have a role to play in helping him decide what to do. I suggested that he talk to our pastor, which he did. While our pastor was sincerely interested in helping Chris, ultimately it still was up to Chris to work it through.

It occurred to me that if our national church organization was sending medical people overseas to help in our world mission program, why couldn't it provide enough supplemental financial aid to Chris to carry out his ministry to the poor people? I communicated with our national church office in Chris's behalf. Nothing could be done. While the program of the church did include financial support for doctors overseas and for lay workers engaged in work with congregations in the United States, there had never been any consideration of supporting laypersons with ministries outside the structure of the church. Chris's ministry just didn't seem to fit into the programs of his church.

Chris finally decided to take the leap. How he did it and how exciting and exhausting his ministry became is a story in itself. He is still struggling to make ends meet financially, but all of his children have been able to go to college, and all of them have chosen medicine as their field!

I cannot talk to Chris without being deeply moved by a layman who has truly found a ministry in his work. Unlike the interns who slapped a bandage on a patient and put him back on the streets again, Chris set out to treat the whole person. "I kept seeing the same people with the same problems being wheeled into the emergency room time after time," he exclaimed. And so he began to work with the welfare people and social service agencies in trying to get at the root causes of the problems of many of his patients. As he helped them to find jobs or secure counseling, he began to minister to the poor in a way totally unlike anything they had experienced with the hospital before. The work is physically exhausting and emotionally draining, but you know that here is a man with real purpose in life.

What about the church? Just as it was not able to help Chris begin his new ministry to people, it has been unable to support him in any meaningful way. People are glad to see Chris and his family at worship and they still ask him to help teach Sunday School. But when it comes to being supportive of Chris's exciting ministry on the emergency floor of a big city hospital, it's almost as if he had decided to become a shoe salesman. Very few know and very few care.

The incredibly ironic part of Chris's ministry is that if he had decided to do exactly the same thing he is now doing, but had undertaken it in a hospital in Africa, the church would have had a keen interest in discussing the matter with him. Assuming the right openings were available, Chris could very well have been sent out by the church as a medical lay worker to minister to blacks overseas. But because he chose to minister to the blacks in America, blacks whose ancestors were brought from Africa in chains to be slaves, his church not only has no provision for supporting his ministry, it actually fails to recognize that what he is doing is a lay ministry. Indeed, at times Chris feels obliged to apologize to his local church leaders about the fact that he is too tired physically to undertake some of the congregational jobs requested of him.

Something is missing. The Eli Blacks, the Nancy Smiths, the Julies, and the Chris Waynes are simply not getting the type of support they need from their religious communities as they strive to relate their faith to their life in personal styles of ministry.

What is wrong? Is it that our churches are so dedicated to institutional goals that they really don't care about the lay-people? Is it that our churches don't know how to help laypeople relate faith to life? Or is it that they don't even know that the problem exists?

2.

THE RHYTHM
OF
CHRISTIAN LIFE

It is interesting to observe the ways in which Jesus used the words "come" and "go."

In Matthew, when he calls Peter and Andrew to be his disciples, Jesus says, "Come with me, and I will make you fishers of men" (Matt. 4:19; NEB). In the Book of Luke, he concludes his magnificent parable of the good Samaritan with the instruction: "Go and do likewise" (Luke 10:37).

Again in Matthew we hear Jesus say, "Come to me, all who labor and are heavy laden, and I will give you rest" (Matt. 11:28). Then when he sends the Seventy out into the world he says, "Go your way; behold, I send you out as lambs in the midst of wolves" (Luke 10:3).

As he pictures the Last Judgment, Jesus says, "Come, O blessed of my Father, inherit the kingdom prepared for you from the foundation of the world" (Matt 25:34). And then, Matthew's last recorded words of Jesus in his appearance after the Resurrection have him saying to his followers, "Go therefore and make disciples of all nations, baptizing them in the name of the Father and of the Son and of the Holy Spirit, teaching them to observe all that I have commanded you" (Matt. 28:19).

Without doubt, there is a consistent pattern in Jesus' use of the words "come" and "go." People are invited to come into a relationship with him in which something is expected to happen. As a result of that encounter with Jesus the eyes of the follower will open to a new way of life. The association with him will enable the believer to receive the teachings, power, and inspiration which will ultimately produce a new person.

But along with the invitation to "come" is the ever present instruction to "go." Once people have seen the vision they are commanded to go and minister to others in the same way that Jesus ministered to them. His final instructions to those who were with him until the very end of his life were to go into the world on his behalf.

The invitation to come to receive his ministering, and the instruction to go to minister to others clearly mark the style of life Jesus establishes for those who believe in him. The New Testament cannot be read otherwise.

The Christian church, in all its denominational variations, has been consistent in claiming that it is the living body of Christ; for two thousand years the church has been the channel for keeping alive the real presence of Christ in human affairs. The church's definition of who it is should largely determine how it functions. If it claims to be the living body of Christ then it should function in the style of Jesus.

There seems to be no argument on this point, either. While it is sometimes difficult to translate the style of Jesus into specific twentieth-century actions, the yardstick of the church's self-evaluation is not in doubt. Ultimately the question is, "How would the style and message of Jesus be applied to current situations?" Admittedly, we often fail. We often inject the will of man into an institutional structure which we claim exists to express the will of God. But what we are talking about here is the theory, the way we say it should be. And clearly we say that the church should function in a manner consistent with the style and teaching of Jesus.

One of the characteristics of the church's life, therefore, should be the gathering and scattering of those who would follow Christ. At all levels of institutional church structure there should be a dedication to the principle that we function in such a way that the followers are gathered together to receive the power of the living Christ and then are scattered to be the agents of sharing that power with others.

The rhythm of gathering and scattering, of coming and going is of course not at all a new concept for the church. Luther certainly articulated such a process as he described how the faithful are to gather for worship, study, and receiving the Word and sacraments so that they are able to go out to be "little Christs" in society. In more recent years many writers and theologians have advocated the same view. Hans-Ruedi Weber, for example, specifically speaks of this rhythm of gathering and scattering as characteristic of the operating style of a congregation of believers.

Frederick K. Wentz in his book *The Layman's Role Today* says: "Our definition of the church ought to describe it as a fellowship of believers who assemble and then disperse, moving out from preaching and sacraments to carry the Word to the world. The church must be a catapult that hurls Christ-bearers into every distant corner of human society."

There have been times in the history of the church when the faithful felt compelled to withdraw totally from the world. Many of the monastic orders placed heavy emphasis on isolation from the secular world. It is debatable whether these movements within the history of the church were an expression or a denial of the ever-living presence of Christ in society. It can be left to others to argue this point.

To put it plainly, the purpose of a congregation today is to provide a means of gathering the believers together for worship, study, receiving of the Word and sacraments, and for mutual inspiration and support *so that* they can go into their daily lives as ministers for Christ. The congregational programs for gathering, therefore, are not ends in themselves; they are a means to an end. The effectiveness of a local congregation should be measured by both the degree to which people are gathered to receive the teachings and power of Jesus *and* the degree to which those same people go out to share that power with others through their own styles of ministry.

How faithful are most congregations to the gathering and scattering rhythm of the Christian life? Not very. The evidence is overwhelming that most congregations of main-line Christian denominations concentrate almost exclusively on those programs which gather the believers and virtually ignore programs which scatter them.

Anyone who has spent time working for his or her local congregation will recognize the obvious ways in which we state our priorities. For example, one of the most common measures of the success of a worship experience or educational program or any other type of gathering has to do with—"How many came?"

"What kind of program will get the most people to come out?" The question is frequently voiced when church groups plan future events. In twenty-five years of working on congregational committees, I've never heard that question rephrased: "What kind of program will help the most people to *go* out?"

In congregation after congregation the so-called Evangelism Committee is almost exclusively concerned with new-member recruitment and with efforts to revitalize the interest of members whose participation in congregational life has been fading. It is extremely unusual to find an Evangelism Committee giving equal concern to helping members articulate their faith in daily life.

Indeed, the universal measure of a vital, active congregation is involvement: all is well when "everyone" is involved in "the work of the church"—which is defined as singing in the choir, teaching Sunday School, ushering at worship, or serving on a committee. As Nancy Smith discovered, a believer who is busy expressing her ministry outside the structure of the parish is made to feel guilty or is abandoned by her fellow believers in that congregation.

Congregational stewardship programs ("stewardship" is usually a code word for parish fund raising) encourage the laity to be more generous givers of time, talents, and money. Seldom is the recipient of this outpouring of giving anything other than the congregation itself. I've never been involved in a parish steward-ship campaign where the laity were urged to pledge contributions for their personal giving to needs outside the walls of the parish as well as within. If giving is in the style of Christian living, then shouldn't congregational leaders be urging members to give wherever they live and work, not just to their local parish?

What is a lay minister? Most people define a lay minister as one who, while not an ordained clergyman, performs such clerical duties in the parish as assisting at worship, teaching, possibly preaching at times, calling on congregational sick and shut-ins, and helping with the administration of the parish. A lay minister is generally considered to be a para-clergyman. Few members of a congregation would ever define a lay minister as a believer who relates his Sunday faith to his weekday life in such a manner as to develop a style of ministry to others beyond the boundaries of his congregation.

I have done a bit of speaking to church groups for many years. It is interesting to note how often both clergy and laypersons say to me, "You ought to be a minister." To this I usually reply, "I am a minister. I am constantly trying to minister to the needs of others." Invariably the response comes back, "No, I mean a *real* minister." We are unable to picture a ministry of laity extending beyond the structure of the religious institution.

Another measure of the way in which the church has emphasized the gathering rather than the scattering can be seen in the way churchmen are today evaluating the events of the past twenty-five years. Why go back twenty-five years? That in itself provides an interesting clue to the way we think about the church's posture in society. In any evaluation of recent church history it is always necessary, it seems, to begin with the 1950s. The decade of the '50s was the glorious decade of "gathering."

For whatever the reason, Americans were attending church services and supporting new building programs as never before. With the rapid development of suburban residential communities, new congregations were being formed all across our nation. Churchgoing was more than a socially acceptable thing; it was culturally necessary.

Recollections of the '50s bring to mind the many ways in which laypersons were called to support the church. There was the obvious need for money for bricks and mortar. But with new and growing congregations there was the need for large numbers of volunteers to teach, to sing, to usher, to serve on the multitudes of committees. The call was for the laypeople to serve the church, not for the church to serve the laypeople where they were.

Then came the 1960s with its wave after wave of "movements." Like the breakers on the shore, a new movement was seen to be developing before the earlier one had even crested. The civil rights movement, with its bus boycotts, restaurant sit-ins, and freedom rides and marches, was in full bloom as the decade opened. Following close behind was the antiwar movement. Closely associated with these two was a rising unrest on college campuses, and the subsequent changes in lifestyle which flowed from the counterculture movement. Towards the latter half of the decade, the ecology movement was making its mark on our society, and as the '60s drew to a close the women's liberation movement was sweeping the nation.

The various church denominations in America responded to the decade of the movements in two distinct ways: they either tried to become involved or they sought to keep aloof. By and large it was the main-line denominations which sought to find ways to relate to the social, political, and economic events of the day while the younger, smaller "evangelistic" sects concentrated on personal salvation.

As the decade of the '60s unfolded, it became increasingly

apparent that the total constituency of the main-line denominations did not wholeheartedly support efforts to have the church relate to the agenda being written by society. And while it is difficult to gauge the impact which church efforts had on the movements, there can be no doubt that many denominations were making a real try for it.

The civil rights movement was personified in a Baptist clergyman, Martin Luther King, Jr. Main-line church representatives, both clergy and lay, rode the freedom buses, marched from Selma, organized fair housing groups, and began new ministries in the poverty-ridden ghettos of our cities. Antiwar rallies generally brought out many young people and a fairly high percentage of church representatives among the older generations. Here again, a movement was somewhat personified by ordained church persons—the Berrigan brothers and Sister Mary McAlister.

Similarly, the issues of counterculture, ecology, women's liberation, the criminal justice system, and the economic order all found the main-line churches striving to relate in some meaningful way. Again, while the impact may not have been great, the fact remains that certain leadership elements in these denominations felt a need for the church to be called to serve man instead of calling men to serve the church.

On the other hand, the younger, smaller, "evangelical" denominations maintained an almost universal posture of non-involvement in the social-political affairs of the nation. Stressing a pietistic, inward-looking style of personal salvation, these smaller denominations seemed to ignore totally the swirl of social change occurring around them. As a matter of fact, it is fair to say that these denominations generally maintained a stance against the movements and for the status quo. The religious leaders who received the warmest welcome in the White House were largely from those denominations which stressed personal piety and ignored the social issues of the day. The Rev. Billy Graham is the personification of this group.

As the American religious establishment moved into the 1970s there was opportunity to reflect upon the recent past and evaluate the two courses taken by the churches in the '60s. The facts were clear enough for anyone to read. Membership growth in the main-line denominations had failed to keep up with population growth rates. Funding had failed to keep up with inflation. There were specific instances where segments of a denomination had intentionally withheld moral and financial support from programs of their church because they did not agree with the philosophy of involvement in the affairs of the world. On the other hand, the pietistic denominations had flourished in terms of membership and financial support as if it were the 1950s all over again.

For many churchmen the conclusion was obvious: emphasis upon the gathering ot the faithful for worship produced "good" results, while sending out the faithful into the complex society in which we live produced "bad" results. One has to ask if that was the yardstick which Jesus used.

The signals are clear, however. After the bruising experiences of the 1960s, main-line denominations are returning to an emphasis on the gathering. Neither the professional leadership nor the loyal lay membership of the main-line denominations is willing to continue to pay the cost of scattering their resources into the affairs of society.

The history of the American religious establishment over the past twenty-five years provides those who are most concerned about church survival with reason enough why churches should concentrate on the gathering of the faithful and not get too involved in the scattering process. Gathering pays off in institutional growth; scattering threatens institutional survival.

But again one has to ask if the same might not have been said about Jesus' ministry. Shouldn't he have been more careful? Wasn't it his very involvement with the outside world which brought about his death? Why did he have to proclaim who he was to others? Why didn't he keep a low profile, gather many followers, and protect them from involvement in the world? How can the church, if it is to have any integrity, live with the contradiction between Jesus' style of gathering and scattering and the present-day concentration on gathering alone?

The church has long suffered under a great self-delusion. For years the leadership of our churches has assumed that if you have adequate programs for gathering, the faithful will just naturally find the effective means for relating their faith to the outside world. If worship is inspiring, if sound sermons are preached, if the sacraments are rightly administered, if there is a good Christian education program, if everyone is somehow involved in the busywork of the local parish, it is assumed that the only logical result is that then the members will go out to relate their faith to their daily lives. The assumption is not correct and survey after survey shows that the self-delusion is pervasive.

In January, 1971, a committee of the National Council of Churches presented the results of a "Listening-to-Lay People Project." The project, begun in 1968, sought to obtain from laypersons their thinking on how the church supported them in their relationships in the world. Over 400 lay participants were enlisted from all parts of the country. They represented an ecumenical and social diversity.

The all-lay participants were asked to address themselves to the following question: "What should the institutional church do to help lay people do what they as responsible Christians should be doing in their occupational, political, social, and other in-the-world relationships and responsibilities?" The inescapable conclusion which must be drawn after reading the study report is that the institutional churches are not helping their laypeople relate their faith to their life in any meaningful way.

Problems began to surface early in the conduct of the survey. The people who handled the many interviews which became the basis of the report discovered that the very concept of the church helping the laity to minister rather than the laity helping to minister to the church was completely foreign to the lay Christian's thinking. While most of the respondents recognized that the institutional church *ought* to be able to help them as lay Christians to live out their faith more effectively in their daily lives, they had never before even considered *how* it could. The report evaluates this situation with the terse statement, "At this point, we believe, the church has abandoned them."

The report says: "Lay people continue to see themselves in their expected role of servants of the institutional church. No one proposed that the church should see its major task to encourage and enable its laypeople to function as crucial change agents in the various institutions in which they live and work. So accustomed are laypeople to turning to the church as the place where they live out their faith, that they go on separating their secular lives from their faith. They worship God in their churches, and serve the churches as best they can both in their institutions and service projects. But they do not find, nor seem to expect, much inspiration or guidance from the church at the most crucial level of their lives—where they carry out their daily work and influence. So, as their despair about the world deepens, the church becomes increasingly irrelevant to what really matters to them." Further on in the report is this appeal from laypeople: "We need a supportive ministry from the church which can nourish our faith and help us take up our roles in secular society as Christians."

The report went on to list various strategies for starting an effective lay ministry program. A budget was proposed. Priorities were listed. What happened to the recommendations? Nothing. Why? Perhaps the reason can be found in an observation which the report itself makes: "The National Council of Churches is a clerically dominated instrument."

In 1972, the Lutheran Church in America at its national convention in Dallas called for a two-year study on "Affirmations of Faith." The action was taken because of a general concern that the members of the LCA needed to reflect upon who they were and what their faith was all about. The convention resolution read in part that the purpose would be "to provide affirmations of faith that will state the church's reason for being and that will help motivate this church to understand and fulfill its mission."

Again, as in the "Listening-to-Lay People" study, the basis of this report was an extensive grass-roots survey of the membership of the LCA. The results of the survey may have been a bit of a surprise to the leadership of the denomination, but they were entirely predictable, based on the earlier study by the National Council of Churches. The report of the Consulting Committee on Affirmations of Faith was presented to the 1974 convention of the LCA in Baltimore. As a result of its extensive surveys, and many conversations with average lay members, the committee found: "The participants (a) believe in Christ, and (b) believe they should serve the world, but (c) wonder how Christ relates to the world."

As one reads the report, one is struck by the evidence of a fundamental gap between the Sunday confessed theology of the laypeople and the weekday operational theologies they carry with them. And, quite obviously, the church is not helping them to close that gap. The report even hints of an institutional fear if that gap between faith and life is permitted to continue, when it warns, "If we do not help our people to put their Sunday and Monday worlds together, sects will attract more and more away."

The Christian church of today must be measured in its fidelity to the style of Jesus who gathered the faithful to receive power and scattered the faithful to spread that power. At what point there is a proper balance between the calling together and the sending out will always be a matter of opinion. But based on the way the church has evaluated itself, based on the nature of its programs, based on its analysis of the role of the church in society over the past twenty-five years, and based on many surveys which reveal the struggle of laypeople to connect their faith to life, one can only conclude that the institutional church has overemphasized the gathering of the faithful at the expense of the scattering of the faithful. The evidence is overwhelming.

3.

CHRISTIANITY
AND
REAL LIFE

Earnest Seal is the new custodian of a large church in Baltimore. He took early retirement from his job at another big steel company because he got so discouraged trying to supervise people who neither wanted to work nor cared about the quality of their product. Once you talk to Earnest and hear his philosphy of life you realize that here is a man who is genuine. He comes across as an honest, hard-working man who values quality as the fruits of his labor.

Earnest was so upset about the work attitudes of the men he had to supervise and so discouraged with his own inability to instill in them the kind of values which he felt were important that he decided to look around for another job and take early retirement. He was encouraged about the possibilities of becoming the custodian of a neighborhood church. In such a job he would work alone and not have to hassle with indifferent subordinates. Moreover, he alone would be responsible for the end result and he could insure quality of workmanship.

Anyone who views the grounds and interior of First Lutheran Church will confirm that Earnest indeed has been able to achieve his objective. The results of his work are magnificent.

The first time I met Earnest, I complimented him on the excellent care he was giving to the church property. It was then that he told me about his reasons for retiring early. He talked about his philosophy of life, and concluded with a statement that continues to haunt me: "I remember what Paul said, that 'whatever you do, do it for the glory of God.' I suppose he was speaking about Christianity, but I think it can apply in real life as well."

Christianity and "real life." Are they separate? Are they two different worlds? Is this the faith of Jesus? Why does a devout, hard-working, churchgoing man like Earnest Seal approach the twilight of his life convinced that he lives in two different worlds, Christianity and real life?

Earnest solved his problem of relating faith and life by deciding to serve the church. The sad truth is that the church failed to serve Earnest, and a group of workers at his former company are probably worse off because of it.

How could his church have helped Earnest Seal? It could have shown him that, as a committed Christian, he had a vital ministry where he was—with his fellow workers in the steel plant. The proclamation of that fact in three or four sermons a year is not enough. Such proclamation becomes authentic only when lay-people actually see their life as an opportunity for ministry, and this comes about only when the church deals with the subject in specific terms and provides the means for encouraging and supporting such ministry.

Suppose a congregation such as the one Earnest Seal belonged to had an annual commissioning service in which various laypersons were appointed to specific types of ministry in their daily lives. Suppose such a congregation provided the means whereby Christian persons in occupations similar to that of Earnest could meet together regularly to discuss their ministries and to support each other as concrete situations arose and had to be dealt with. Suppose a pastor sat in on such meetings to learn more about the real-life problems of people like Earnest and to provide theological support for the various dimensions of these lay ministries. Suppose the congregation belonged to a denomination where laypeople were given help in developing special skills for ministry, were taught how to listen, how to evaluate interpersonal problems, how to communicate the faith. Would such efforts make a difference in the lives of laypeople like Earnest Seal? Of course they would.

In subsequent chapters we will deal with a wide range of possibilities for lay ministry. We will also deal with ways in which the institutional church can develop and support such ministries. But detailed examples of lay ministries and the means to achieve them will be better understood if further consideration is first given to the concept of lay ministry and to the inherent institutional barriers which effectively impede such ministries.

The synoptic Gospels all report how Jesus sent out the twelve disciples, two by two, to expand his ministry by reaching and serving others. In Luke, for example, we read, "Jesus called the twelve disciples together and gave them power and authority to drive out all demons and to cure diseases. Then he sent them out to preach the Kingdom of God and to heal the sick" (Luke 9:1). Here again is an example of the gathering of the faithful to receive power and the scattering of the faithful to spread that power among the people.

In today's terms the twelve disciples could be considered nothing more nor less than laypersons. They had not been formally trained to be ministers of God. They had not been ordained into a professional calling of the church. They were followers of Jesus—believers, just as we all are. They were "called together" by Jesus, just as the church, the living body of Christ, calls the faithful together today. Luke says they were given "power and authority to drive out all demons and to cure diseases." It is at this point that laypeople today frequently want to break off any comparison between their ministries and those of the Twelve. Perhaps the problem lies in our understanding of the "demons" and "diseases."

Do we understand that word "demon" only in terms of the "evil spirt" which inhabited the young boy and threw him into a

fit, as recorded in the ninth chapter of Luke? Do we think of
"diseases" as primarily leprosy? Or can we see that our society
today is beset with all kinds of demons and that our brothers and
sisters are afflicted with all kinds of diseases which desperately
need the healing power of Jesus? Have we been given the power
to dispel the demons and diseases of our modern society?
According to the varying gifts we have, the answer must be yes.
To say no is to deny the presence of Christ in our lives and the
power which can flow from him, through us, to others.

It is also interesting to note that when Jesus sent out the
Twelve, he sent them two by two. Again in the tenth chapter of
Luke, when Jesus sends out the Seventy, he sends them two by
two. Jesus knew what the modern church appears to have
forgotten: laypeople need some organized structure for supporting each other in ministry. Who started the original Christian
support groups? Jesus did.

The letters of Paul clearly indicate that the early church
seriously dealt with the ministry of all believers. Paul's treatment
of lay ministry offers basic points that are absolutely essential for
a responsible ministry of laypeople in society today. Perhaps
foremost among them is the recognition of "gifts."

Paul writes: "There are different kinds of spiritual gifts, but
the same Spirit gives them. There are different ways of serving,
but it is the same Lord who is served. There are different abilities
to perform service, but it is the same God who gives ability to
everyone for all services. Each one is given some proof of the
Spirit's presence for the good of all. The Spirit gives one man the
power to work miracles; to another the gift of speaking God's
message; and to yet another, the ability to tell the difference
between gifts that come from the Spirit and those that do not. To
one man he gives the ability to speak with strange sounds; to
another he gives the ability to explain what these sounds mean.
But it is one and the same Spirit who does all this; he gives a
different gift to each man as he wishes" (1 Cor. 12:4-11; TEV).

Paul then goes on to describe the body of Christ as being made up of many members. Just as the human body depends upon its different parts, so the body of Christ depends upon the abilities and functions of its various members.

The theme is repeated in the letter to the Ephesians. "It was he who 'gave gifts to men'; he appointed some to be apostles, others to be prophets, others to be evangelists, others to be pastors and teachers. He did this to prepare all God's people for the work of Christian service, to build up the body of Christ" (Eph. 4:11; TEV).

It seems that the church of today has not helped laypeople to identify their gifts. On the contrary, as Nancy Smith discovered, a gift which leads a committed Christian into service beyond the limits of congregational life is discouraged.

In the modern church gifts are identified only to the extent of finding talented persons who can sing in the choir, those who are "good at working with the youth," and those who might add prestige or expertise in running the church and its various programs.

Elizabeth O'Connor's *Eighth Day of Creation* deals extensively with the need for all of us to identify our gifts. She points out that the identifying of gifts brings to the fore another large issue in our lives, the issue of commitment. For, once I can clearly see my gift, then the next step is to commit myself to the use of it. And that is the start of my lay ministry.

Martin Luther spoke quite plainly of a universal priesthood of all believers. It was he who called upon laity and clergy alike to become the "little Christs" of society. In the same manner as Jesus ministered to men, so Luther saw all the believers having a universal ministry to others. In one of his better known examples, Luther said, "If you are a craftsman, you will find the Bible placed in your workshop, in your hands, in your heart; it teaches and preaches how you ought to treat your neighbor. Only look at your tools, your needle, your thimble, your beer barrel, your articles of trade, your scales, your measures, and you will find this saying written on them. You will not be able to look anywhere where it does not strike your eyes. None of the things with which you deal daily are too trifling to tell you this incessantly, if you are but willing to hear it; and there is no lack of such preaching for you have as many preachers as there are transactions, commodities, tools, and other implements in your house and estate; and they shout this to your face, 'My dear, use me toward your neighbor as you would want him to act toward you with that which is his.' "

When survey after survey reveals the fact that the churches are not helping the laity to relate their faith to their daily lives, one might be tempted to conclude that somehow in recent years the concept of lay ministry has been lost. Yet this is not at all true. The call for a more direct relationship of faith to life for all Christians has been a common theme in the recent writings of religious authors and commentators.

Hans-Ruedi Weber, in his book *Salty Christians,* and Hendrik Kraemer, in his book *A Theology of the Laity,* bring into sharp focus the way in which Christians should be bringing their faith to bear upon the life situations they face. Mark Gibbs and Ralph Morton, noted English authors, have co-authored provocative books on the role of the laity, *God's Frozen People* and *God's Lively People.*

During the 1960s there was a flood of books in which the institutional church was severely castigated for many things, not the least of which was its self-centeredness and inability to direct its thinking to the involvement of laypeople in their daily lives. In *The Noise of Solemn Assemblies,* Peter Berger said, "The sharp edge of the Christian engagement with the modern world is not likely to be in the parish." In *Honest To God,* John Robinson said: "That Christianity should be equated in the public mind, inside as well as outside the church, with 'organized religion' merely shows how far we have departed from the New Testament. For the last thing the church exists to be is an organization for the religious. Its charter is to be the servant of the world." Similarly, Colin Morris in his book *Include Me Out* wrote, "But what is beyond doubt is that Jesus' first recorded demand upon men was not that they should worship him or theologize about him, or build a Church around him, but that they should follow him."

One could go on and on with citations about the religious institutions being too much church-centered and not enough world-centered, but the point has been made. The disciples of Jesus were "sent out" to minister. Paul prized the gifts that made for distinctive ministries. Luther emphasized the universal priesthood of all believers. And modern religious writers and theologians continue to call for world-centered styles of ministry.

Yet in the face of all this, most lay members of our churches today maintain that the church is *not* helping them to relate their faith to their life.

Why?

4.

ROLES
AND
RESOURCES

In their book, *God's Lively People,* Mark Gibbs and Ralph Morton comment on the inability of the church to develop ministries of the laity in their daily lives: "It is also clear that many of the hopes in Britain, in Europe, and in North America about a renewal of the laity have come to nothing. Despite the writing and teaching of Hendrik Kraemer, Hans-Ruedi Weber, Franklin Littell, and other distinguished teachers in the lay movement, many laypeople have been unable to hold together a live membership in the church and a genuine involvement in the affairs of the world. Some of them, especially in Britain, have finally lost hope in the institutional churches; those now left in the pews are often churchy laity who are as ecclesiastical as any arch deacon."

Is such a statement equally true of the situation in America? In my opinion it is, but because of a more active lay involvement in the institutional housekeeping of the church the American problem is even more complex.

At the risk of oversimplification, there are two areas of the problem which appear not to have been seriously dealt with: roles and resources. The roles of both the clergy and the laity must be carefully considered if lay ministries are to develop. Moreover, the resources for the enabling of such ministries may very well not be where people have been looking for many years. It is highly important to consider both of them.

The matter of roles comes most clearly into focus when controversy arises within a congregation. Controversy may arise out of differences over worship, educational programs, or finances, but it is most frequently encountered when the church tries to deal with social concerns. From the smallest parish to the national offices of the largest denomination, the manner in which the church has responded (or failed to respond) to the social issues of the day has been the single most fertile field for controversy. "Religion and politics don't mix" is a maxim which has quite obviously been drawn from experience.

As we have moved around the country, Judy and I have served on a number of local congregational committees charged with carrying out the social ministry of our church. Our experiences have been repeated so many times and in so many places that it is perfectly safe to generalize on the roles which are played out during periods of controversy in a congregation.

It goes something like this: At any given time there are current issues facing our nation which seem to be of considerable interest to almost everyone. It may be corruption in local or national government, civil rights, war, crime and the justice system, abortion, the counterculture, or liberation movements. The list we've gone through in the past twenty years is lengthy.

Any clergyman worth his salt feels that his parishioners should be helped to see their religion in terms of their daily life situations. And so he quite often will weave into his sermons a theological perspective for those issues which seem to be before the nation at the time. On some issues, such as discrimination, there is little choice as to what position the preacher will take if he is at all true to his calling as a man of God. Some clergy are very bold in their prophetic roles; others are more conciliatory. Not all the parishioners will approve of the preacher's position, but usually there is little more than complaints and grumbling so long as the issues go no further than the pulpit.

Problems arise when some of the laity see fit to respond to the injustices being chronicled from the pulpit. If the pastor succeeds in awakening the conscience of some of his members, he is then faced with answering the very real question: "Pastor, what can we do?" And once people in the parish begin *doing* things about current social problems, the level of controversy sharply escalates.

The "doers" have been given a cause. Having been stimulated into action by what they have heard from their own religious leaders, the doers' sense of calling and of being on the side of right is often very strong. They make the issues concrete by getting involved with local politicians, or by starting fair housing committees, or by organizing demonstrations to highlight their position.

Meanwhile opposition mounts within the congregation. Some members object to the position being taken by the pastor and the doers. Some object to the very idea that the church should be involved in the affairs of the outside world at all. As the controversy grows, people begin withholding contributions and staying away from church affairs; some even transfer their membership to other congregations.

Sooner or later comes the showdown. The governing body of the congregation, charged with the responsibility of maintaining the existence of the parish, pressures the pastor to tone down his position and to "talk" to those members who are supporting the social cause. On the other hand, the newly stimulated social activists are unhappy that the pastor is not giving them even greater support from the pulpit and more of his personal involvement in the issue. The pastor is caught squarely in the middle.

Under these circumstances, it has been my experience that the pastor sees his chief responsibility to be the preservation of the congregation as an ongoing group. Few pastors are willing to support a social cause to the point where it totally destroys the congregation—nor am I suggesting they should. I must admit that there have been times when I have been bitterly disappointed that one of my pastors put the survival of the congregation above an issue which, to me, seemed so fundamental to the Christian faith. Were they hypocrites? I don't think so. Were they afraid? Perhaps.

In retrospect I have come to understand that the problem is simply one of role identification. Our clergy are called to lead congregations into areas of greater growth. Their entire professional training is in the areas which serve to gather the believers together to receive the Word and sacraments. The more people who are reached by their ministries, the more there are who can follow the Christian life. All the measures of success are in terms of growth in membership, participation, and finances. Is it so surprising that when a pastor is forced to choose between working to gather the people and working to scatter them in society, he generally chooses the former?

Cop out? Cowardice? Hypocrisy? Such words can be tossed at pastors all to easily. Could it be that good, honest people have been given roles so broad that they cannot possibly be held responsible for both the gathering and the scattering of the members of their congregations?

What is true at the local parish level is equally true at the level of the national church organizations. While some departments of the denomination are engaged in activities that bring the church into the affairs of the world, by far the largest commitments of time, staff, and resources are directed to those activities which strengthen the organization itself.

Pierre Berton, in his book *The Comfortable Pew,* issued a scathing denunciation of the church's tendency toward concentrating on maintaining the institution: "In short, the maintenance of the religious establishment has become an end in itself, and not a means, something more important than Christian principle, Christian action, or even Christian brotherhood.''

It is useless to debate whether the situation described is right or wrong—the description is true. The leadership of our churches, both clergy and lay, at both the local and national levels, see their primary roles as guardians of the institution. It is a waste of time to talk about changing that. We must accept the fact and go on from there.

In any discussion of the ministry of the laity, the question is invariably asked why the lay leadership of the institutional church does not itself become the nucleus of a lay renewal movement. However, when one considers the roles that laypeople play within the church, it can be seen that generally the vision of lay leadership also is focused on the church instead of the world.

Mark Gibbs distinguishes between two kinds of laity in making this very point. He says there is one group of laity, which he labels "Type A," who have their interests in the world outside the church. These laity are active in their careers, in local or national politics, in various voluntary civic organizations, and in their homes and family lives. Laity "Type B" have their main interest in life centered on their church and its organization. They serve on committees, teach Sunday School, sing in choirs, raise funds, and call on new members.

It is the Type B laity who are in the lay leadership positions of the local congregations, the regional conferences or districts, and the national boards. It is the layperson who has faithfully served his congregation who is nominated to attend regional conventions. Loyal service on regional committees will be rewarded by election or appointment to national boards and conventions. And loyal support of the institution results in remaining in the assignment or being named to another responsibility if the first office happens to have a limited term of service.

I am a member of the Executive Council of the Lutheran Church in America. The council consists of thirty members elected by our national convention for terms of four years. Half the members are ordained clergy; the other fifteen are laypersons. But every one of the laypersons has served many years at the congregational and synodical levels of our church structure. Some of our so-called lay members are actually on the payroll of the church, serving in such positions as assistant to a synod president, teacher in a seminary, or employee of a church-related college.

These are all good, dedicated people who unselfishly give much service to the church. They are needed. We can be thankful that the church has such lay leadership. But the council's vision is primarily church-centered rather than world-centered. If there is to be a true movement to help laypeople in the congregations relate their faith to their life in the real world, its nucleus cannot come from lay leadership whose vision is primarily church-centered.

As a matter of fact, when I talk to my associates in the church, both lay and clergy, about the two different worlds of men like Earnest Seal, many really do not comprehend. For the clergy, their "real life" *is* the church. There is no gap to straddle. For the Type B laity who are active in the church, the problem of relating Sunday faith to Monday life has largely been solved by making the church their major focus of interest. Despite all the surveys, a few of my lay friends on the Executive Council do not agree that our laypeople have a problem relating faith to life. To them the answer to such a charge is easy: "Tell the laypeople to get more active in their church!"

Any development of lay ministries within the organized church must take into consideration the roles in which both pastors and lay leaders see themselves. Failure to do this will doom any new initiatives, as the past has amply demonstrated.

The second factor which must be considered in evaluating why lay ministries have not developed in the Christian church involves *resources*. What are the resources that have generally been suggested whenever serious consideration is given to lay ministries? The most commonly suggested resource is the parish pastor. Putting aside for the moment the problem of role identity of the parish pastor, let's test the suggestion that he is the obvious initial resource for developing lay ministries.

The parish pastor relates to the people in his congregation in several ways. He reaches the largest number of people through his preaching. A smaller number is reached through personal counseling. In terms of the administration of the affairs of the congregation, his contacts with laypeople are of such a nature that the agenda which brings them together, be it committee work, fund raising or whatever, generally precludes any possibility for discussion of lay ministries. Generally speaking, therefore, the average pastor is able to communicate with the laypeople only—or mainly—through his sermons and through personal counseling. How effective are these channels?

Peter Berger is quite caustic in his evaluation of the effect of preaching on the lives of the people: "Since the religious institutions are prominent and prosperous, it is only natural for the religious functionaries to assume that what they say and do has great impact upon the lives of the people. The most common delusion in this area is the conviction of ministers that what they preach on Sunday has a direct influence on what their listeners do on Monday. This conviction, because it is so important for the self-image of the minister, is adhered to despite mountains of evidence to the contrary."

The preacher starts with the theology and then works it into examples of real-life situations. The layperson starts with the real-life situation and then has a need for the theology which applies to it. The difference is crucial.

For many years I have been concerned with finding effective ways to communicate the basis of my faith orally when a real-life situation seemed to call for a personal sharing of it. I have found that too often the language of the church not only has been inadequate to fit the situation, but that it often causes others to shut the door on communication. And so, I'm always interested in listening to sermons on communicating the faith—on evangelism as many of us call it.

Not long ago, I heard such a sermon. It was given by a minister who was an excellent scholar and an effective speaker. I was solidly with him as he developed the biblical basis and rationale for an oral communication of our faith. He was good, very good. Having developed a strong case on the basis of our theology, he turned to the real-life practical application. Looking out across the congregation, with great passion he threw out this challenge: "Next time someone asks you why you are a Christian, what will you say?" My heart sank. I sighed in keen disappointment. That was not the right question. In all the years of work and travel in my career as a businessman, in all those conferences, at all those business meals, on all those plane trips, not once did anyone ever ask me why I was a Christian. Associates of mine who were aware of some of the things we were doing in our lives may have asked why we were doing them, and thereby may have offered an opportunity for discussion of the faith, but I've never heard the direct question asked the way the preacher seemed to think is perfectly commonplace. The real question is, "How does a layperson initiate a discussion relating to his faith without immediately turning off the other person?" I thought about the letdown of that sermon for several days. Was that minister so removed from the reality of lay experience that he didn't realize the inappropriateness of his question? Or was he so intent on the theological basis of his message that he really didn't care to seek out a valid practical application? Whatever the reason, here was an excellent preacher, a sound theologian, who simply was not able to relate his material to the life situations of the people he was addressing.

Part of the problem, of course, is that most clergymen have not had any years of experience in a career outside the church. Those men who have had a prior career before entering the ministry have somewhat of an advantage in this respect.

Another part of the problem is to be found in the short-comings of a monologue sermon. A dialogue style in which laypeople are able to respond and ask questions is more effective. What is most effective is when laypeople are wrestling with a life situation and the minister is able to bring into the discussion the appropriate theological and scriptural considerations. But then we don't call that a sermon, do we? The sermon, as we now know it, is not at all an effective way of encouraging and supporting laypeople's ministries in life.

Counseling is a better method, but here again, the pastor's experiential limitations exist, and he does not have the time to counsel individually with all the laity of the congregation. Could we expect any pastor to be qualified to counsel his laypeople in all their real-life situations, even if he had the time to do it? I don't think so, because so many of our problem areas as laypeople involve very complex situations which extend beyond the professional competence of any one man.

Take for example the issue of price fixing in American industry. The act is so clearly illegal that one can scarcely imagine any circumstance which could cloud the absoluteness of the wrong. It is referred to frequently in sermons as an illustration of the evils of our society.

Many years ago, when I was a young steel salesman in Michigan, I experienced a situation involving attempted price fixing. The federal highway building program was just getting started, and because I was doing an aggressive job, our company was getting a large share of the available business. One of my competitors was a small steel distributor. The owner, a man in his sixties, had worked very hard to get his company to where it was. He had literally poured his life into that business. He had reason to be proud of what he had done. But in recent years it was becoming obvious that his firm was slipping and was being outsold by me and other competitors. Perhaps he was getting too old, or was beginning to coast; I don't know.

One night he called me at my home. I was surprised that he knew where I lived. "Mr. Diehl," he said, "we've got to do something to improve our prices." Before I could say a word in reply, he went into an emotional presentation about how close his business was to bankruptcy. He said that if things continued the way they were going for another six months he would lose everything he had in life. And then he added the clincher: "Mr. Diehl, if that happens, I'm going to kill myself!"

As soon as I could get a word in, I told him I could not agree even to discuss the possibility of meeting to fix prices—it was illegal. He acknowledged that it was, but asked me to think it over for a week. He would call again, he said. And then he closed with another appeal: "How can a young man like you live with yourself knowing that you are destroying me?"

I was stunned. What should I do? I knew it was illegal to do what he asked, but suppose he was in earnest. Suppose in six months he was bankrupt and committed suicide. Would I feel responsible? How could I live with that? Should I turn him in? Would that destroy him? Does he need psychiatric help? How could I make any approach to help him personally without getting deeper into a potential price-fixing mess? Should I be a little less aggressive and let him get more business? Would that be fair to my company? Indeed, if I did hold back, even without agreeing to, couldn't that very act be considered legal evidence of a conspiracy since it was the result of his request? What was legal? What was moral? What did my Christian faith say to this situation? Is the very concept of free enterprise in business consistent with Christianity?

I had a close personal relationship with our parish pastor. We had shared many things together, and he had done a great deal to stimulate my thinking about the faith. He was one of the people I counseled with about the problem. Although our pastor expressed concern and support, he was very honest in saying that he could not provide the kind of professional help I needed. My problem was resolved by talking to my manager, to an attorney, and to several businessmen who were friends in the neighborhood and in the church. From these more experienced men I got a sharper perspective on the laws and on our company policies. I also heard their judgment that I was being used, by a man who was not telling the truth. They were right.

This example illustrates the problem of resources for lay ministries. There was no obvious support group to whom I could turn for help. I had to seek out a half-dozen laymen and explain my predicament to each of them. The pastor did not have the background or experience to deal with the problem from a total perspective. His help consisted primarily in showing me ways in which basic considerations of our faith might relate to my situation. That in itself was helpful, but couldn't there have been a better way of putting it all together? Suppose I had been a member of a small group of businessmen who were meeting regularly to discuss ways in which their Christian faith related to their work, and to support each other in times of crisis? Suppose this group had a clergyman sitting in as a resource person to ask some penetrating questions and provide a degree of theological input. Had such a group existed at the time, securing the resources I needed would have been no problem for me. They would have been readily available in an ongoing group of lay-persons who knew me very well and who would have provided immediate and personal support.

One might conclude that in terms of problem solving my method of rounding up the necessary resources to deal with the suggested price-fixing situation was perfectly adequate. For me that problem was such a severe one that I had to seek out help. But how about the many smaller problems a Christian faces in business every day? Where does one go for resources in dealing with minor business matters that relate to faith? To whom can one address important questions when the pace of work is so fast that many things are done without serious reflection as to their consequences? What occasions are there for a person to sit back and reflect upon one's ministry of life on the job? Who is there to help in such self-evaluation?

Can the layperson get the needed support from a sermon? No. Do the resources currently exist within the local congregation for providing the kind of support laypersons need in relating faith to life? No. Is there any type of structure within the churches of America for providing resources for supporting laypeople in life ministries? With very few exceptions, the answer is again, no.

Who, then, can fill the role of scattering the laity into the world? Who can help us bring Christianity into real life? And who has the resources for enabling such ministries that they might be effective?

In 1965 an ecumenical consultation on laity formation was held at Gazzada, Italy. The event was jointly sponsored by the World Council of Churches' Department on the Laity and the Permanent Committee for International Congresses of the Lay Apostolate (Rome), better known as COPECIAL. A similar consultation subsequently was held in September, 1974, at Assisi. It is important to observe the shift in thinking about lay ministry which occurred during the decade between these consultations.

The 1965 consultation issued the following resolution: "We, the members of the Informal Consultation called jointly by COPECIAL and the Department of Laity of the World Council of Churches, unanimously agree (1) that the training of the laity should be considered as a priority in the policy, program, and allocation of finances of the churches represented and (2) that all suitable opportunities be taken by the Roman Catholic, Orthodox, and Protestant Churches to cooperate together in this field of lay training, and to share insights, personnel, facilities and other resources of movements and centers." Quite obviously, the general direction for lay formation in 1965 was that the church institutions would design and deliver programs for the training of the laity.

A decade later the focus had shifted significantly. One of the prominent trends in the 1974 consultation was the shift in emphasis from the laity as objects of formation to the laity as subjects of formation. The point seemed to surface again and again that "the laity must be agents of their own formation." What this means, according to Frank W. Klos, an LCA participant in the consultation, is "that laity formation begins where people are with their needs, and interests, that they together with specialists shape the kind of training or education or guided experiences they need to deal with the challenges they face in everyday life." Mr. Klos identified a number of trends which seemed to be generally expressed by the broad range of world participants. One of these trends, which we will deal with later in this book, was "the trend toward less participation in and identification with established church organizations and toward more development of unofficial Christian communities gathered for fellowship, support, worship, and service apart from ecclesiastical structures."

"The laity must be agents of their own formation." That's a difficult concept for the institutional church to accept. It is almost immediately taken as an anticlerical statement and evokes rapid defensive reactions.

"More development of unofficial Christian communities apart from the ecclesiastical structure." That's a frightening concept for the insititutional church to accept. It is almost immediately taken as an anti-institutional statement and evokes predictions of chaos and ultimate death of the church.

The opposite prediction may be closer to the truth: The self-formation of the laity and the growth of unofficial Christian communities are necessary steps in the development of lay ministries, and the by-product of such a lay movement will be a revitalization of the institutional church.

Who can best fill the roles and furnish the resources to develop lay ministries? No one but the laity themselves.

5.

THE MINISTRY
OF THE
AID MAN

Advocates of a lay ministry in society frequently use Martin Luther's image of the "little Christ" to illustrate their vision. It was Luther's contention that all followers of Christ, be they clergy or lay, should function wherever they are in the style of Jesus. He did not believe that one vocation was more acceptable in the eyes of God than another. He felt that all people, in whatever endeavor they happened to find themselves, could serve God by bringing his love to others.

If we build upon this image, then how do we define ministry in the style of Jesus? Is it preaching? Is it healing? How broad a range of activity does it cover? How did Jesus define his ministry?

In Luke there is the account of Jesus returning from his period of forty days in the wilderness to begin his ministry. The classic description of his ministry was given in the synagogue in Nazareth when he stood up and read from the Book of Isaiah: "The Spirit of the Lord is upon me, because he has anointed me to preach good news to the poor. He has sent me to proclaim release to the captives, and recovering of sight to the blind, to set at liberty those who are oppressed, and to proclaim the acceptable year of the Lord" (Luke 4:18).

Later in the Gospel of Luke there is the account of messengers being sent by John the Baptist to learn if Jesus was indeed the promised one, or if they should expect someone else. In response to their questions, Jesus answers by defining again the marks of his ministry: "Go and tell John what you have seen and heard: the blind receive their sight, the lame walk, lepers are cleansed, and the deaf hear, the dead are raised up, and the poor have good news preached to them" (Luke 7:22).

In this and the next several chapters we will be describing types of lay ministries which involve such activity. We will speak of healing, proclamation of the good news, setting free those who are bruised, restoring sight to those who are blind, and proclaiming liberty to captives.

One lay ministry, which is applicable to a wide range of lay activity, is what I choose refer to as the "aid man" of society. I borrowed the term from my military experience.

During the Second World War, I served as a combat medical aid man with a tank batallion of the Tenth Armored Division in Europe. Attached to each batallion was a medical unit consisting of two commissioned officers who were professional physicians or surgeons, plus about twenty noncommissioned officers and men. While some of the non-coms in our unit had civilian experience as pharmacists or para-medics, the vast majority of the enlisted men had no previous experience in the field of medicine.

The two professional doctors and several of the enlisted men comprised the staff of our batallion aid station. The batallion aid station moved from location to location as the front lines advanced, always setting up the treatment facilities close to the center of action. It was the first point of contact that a wounded soldier would have with a professional medical man.

The majority of the enlisted men in the detachment served as medical aid men. Two of us would ride in a litter-bearing jeep and be assigned to a particular tank company during combat. Generally we were on duty with that company for twenty-four hours and then returned to the batallion aid station for twenty-four hours of rest and duty there.

When the tank company was attacking in single file, we usually followed closely behind the last tank in line. When the tanks were dispersed, we tried to position ourselves in the middle where we could observe all the action. We were tuned in on the same radio frequency used by the company commander so we could know what was going on. When one of our tanks was hit by enemy fire and there were injuries, we heard the familiar call, "Medic, front!" We would immediately speed to the disabled tank to determine the extent of injuries.

Battlefield injuries can be of a wide variety. There can be minor burns or severe burns. Injury from shrapnel can involve minor cuts or massive destruction of the body. There can be minor bruises and sprains, or there can be fractured bones and torn ligaments.

If the injury was minor, we had been trained to provide the necessary treatment to enable the man to return to duty. If the injury were serious we placed the man on our litter and got him back to the batallion aid station as fast as possible. There he was treated by professional doctors. While it was very important to move the wounded out of action as fast as possible, it was also very important to know enough about the nature of his injury to keep him alive and prevent the injury from getting worse. We had to be able to treat for shock, stop massive bleeding, immobilize a fracture, give artificial respiration, or utilize other first aid procedures until professional help was available. The training of previously unexperienced men to provide medical aid for wounded soldiers was a key element in the United States Army's achieving a high degree of success in keeping alive the injured.

Combat is a frightening experience. To be wounded in combat is doubly frightening. And so, as best we could, we tried to bring comfort as well as treatment to our wounded. By what we said and the way we worked, we tried to provide assurance that all would be well. Our obvious determination not to let any soldier die while under our care had to be a source of support for the injured. Since we generally knew many of the men in our batallion, we often were able to provide that added degree of support that can come when a friend is by your side. We cared—and the wounded knew it.

Every day all of us move among persons who are hurting in one way or another. The problems facing people in our society are many and diverse. There are medical problems, emotional problems, financial problems, family problems, business problems, interpersonal problems. There are the wounds which come with losing a loved one, with divorce, with retirement, with leaving home. There are the hurts which come with moving to a new location, with the loss of a job, with failure to attain a goal, with rejection by a loved one.

Who is there to help the people who are hurting? Where are the aid men of society? We have doctors, lawyers, psychologists, clergymen, social workers, marriage counselors, and other types of professionals who have been trained to minister to the special needs of people. But just as soldiers wounded in combat do not all end up in a batallion aid station, not every one with a problem in our society needs a professional. In fact, many physicians complain that they are already spending too much time with patients whose only need is to have someone listen to them. On the other hand there are many people who do need professional help but do not get it because no one is there to detect the problem and suggest the referral.

Many of us with friends and family have people to whom we can turn with our hurts and problems. The assistance that we get, however, may or may not be of help. Family and friends may be so busy with their own life situations that they can scarcely attend to our wounds. Or perhaps they sincerely try to be helpful, but their lack of training leaves much to be desired. It's almost as if the army left the front line medical treatment up to the rest of the soldiers. In some cases that might be satisfactory, but in most cases the job of treating the wounded would not be well done.

It seems to me that the Christian community of believers can perform a vital ministry to all of society if lay people in large numbers are called to be the aid men of society—and are given the necessary training to do the job well. What is needed is a network of Christian laypersons who are skilled in the early detection of human problems. For years we have known that the earlier a medical problem is detected, the easier it can be cured; as a result we have made a few feeble steps towards early detection of critical diseases. But the same early detection is needed for all types of human problems—family problems, emotional problems, financial problems—all of them.

This need is being recognized in the development of publicly financed crisis intervention programs in various parts of our country. A close friend of ours has recently been called as the coordinator of a crisis intervention team in a neighboring county. She will supervise three teams, each working an eight-hour shift in order to provide twenty-four-hour service to the citizens of the county. Each team consists of a nurse, a social worker, and a psychologist. They try to assist people in situations where direct professional services are not available or are obviously not needed. For example, suppose a neighbor calls the police to quell a violent argument between a husband and wife. The police answer the call. They come upon a scene of anger and hostility. But no law has been broken, no one has yet been injured, and the safety of others has not been threatened. What are the police to do? Previously they could do little more than issue some stern warnings and leave. Now they call the crisis intervention team. The team will spend time with the family, trying to cool the situation and trying to get to the source of the hostility. Depending upon the origin of the problem, appropriate steps may be taken. Perhaps one of the partners in the marriage is under emotional stress. Perhaps a severe financial problem has triggered the fight. Perhaps a marriage counselor is needed. Whatever the cause, the crisis intervention team will try to bring in appropriate help to prevent the situation from deteriorating further.

Such crisis intervention programs are springing up in many parts of the country. A number of colleges are now offering courses in training for crisis intervention.

Even the business community is beginning to respond to the same type of need among its workers. The May 30, 1975, issue of *American Metal Market* reports on a new program called PACE which was put into operation at the Aeroquip Corporation of Jackson, Michigan. PACE, an acronym for Personal Assistance Committee for Employees, was formed by joint action of the company and the local union of the United Auto Workers. "The purpose of the program is to help employees who might be affected by alcoholism, drug dependence, and other problems such as financial, emotional, or legal hang-ups that might affect job performance," reports the article. If requested, PACE will even offer its assistance to members of an employee's family. The aims and purposes of the program are "to provide an early detection program for problems and to direct troubled employees to sources of help before their problems worsen and cause them to become unemployable." When an employee is referred to PACE there is a private discussion about personal concerns. Confidentiality is strictly maintained. The PACE committee members then seek to determine the general nature of the problem as a first step toward referring the employee to the proper channels of professional help.

If the need for early problem detection is becoming more evident to local governmental agencies and even to business, isn't there a clear call for action on the part of Christian laypersons? A number of times I have heard men complain that their wives seem to get all the problems of the neighborhood dumped on them: "The other women in the neighborhood are forever coming by for a cup of coffee, but they end up unloading all their problems on poor Alice." When the speaker's wife tried to defend what was happening, he put her down. He warned her about getting involved in other people's problems and came very close to asking her to stop it.

What a shame! There are many women like Alice who have a special gift—they are open enough and listen well enough that people with problems will approach them. There are far more opportunities for the ministry of listening and counseling in the breakfast rooms of our homes than there will ever be in the studies of our parish ministers.

Instead of looking at Alice's situation in a negative way, the Christian community should be positive about it. Alice's immediate Christian community should help Alice—and her husband—recognize that she has been give a special gift. The community should help her develop her skills in using this gift. And finally her Christian community should give official recognition to her ministry of listening and counseling in somewhat the same way they give public recognition to their Sunday School teachers, their congregational officers, or their Scoutmaster.

In a sense women with gifts such as Alice has could function as a kind of combat medic in society. A clarification of their role could (a) help them see and build upon special gifts they have been given, (b) give additional purpose to their lives in the sense of a calling to a type of lay ministry, (c) fulfill a needed service in society, and (d) bridge that gap between Sunday faith and the weekday real life.

The aid man type of lay ministry is needed wherever there are people, particularly wherever people relate to one another on a continuing basis.   A file clerk in an office building, a college student among his or her peer group, a supervisor in a manufacturing plant, a high school teacher, the vice-president of a bank, a professional athlete—all represent the wide range of occupations in which aid man ministries are possible.

The requirements of an aid man ministry are remarkably similar to those of combat medics. Several may be mentioned.

First, the lay minister must be available. Like the combat medic, he must be close to where the action is.

But being where the action is, and having access to that action, does not necessarily mean we are available. Just as the combat medic has to have his visual and audio channels of communication open to hear calls for help, so too lay ministers have to keep their communication channels open. Sometimes that is not as easy as it sounds. Sometimes we fool ourselves about our channels being open when they really are not.

Most of my executive associates like to say that they have an "open door" policy in their office. They feel that they have created a climate in which anyone can come into their office and make a suggestion or discuss a problem. Many are kidding themselves. Few business executives have a truly open door policy. They get suggestions all right, but only those the employees think the boss will like. They get reactions to a change in policy, but only after it becomes apparent how the boss himself feels about the policy change. And they seldom get personal problems, since the sharing of a problem may betray a weakness which will affect the evaluation and future of the worker's career. No, most business executives have offices as closed as if they had bars on the door.

To be available as a lay minister means to be truly open and aware. Some individuals have Alice's natural gift of openness. For others the talent can be developed. Sessions in consciousness-raising can help people open their minds and senses to the many things which happen all around them every day. Membership in a small group may provide the psychological support needed to become more open. Within a truly supportive small group we begin to learn how others see us, we are encouraged to experiment with other styles of relating to people, and we receive honest feedback and reinforcement of those personality characteristics which tend to make us more open. The church can support lay ministries by providing experiences in consciousness-raising and encouraging the development of small support groups.

Being open and available for ministry, however, is not enough if we don't know how to listen. Our company, in the training of its professional salesmen, conducts a short course on how to listen. There is often a difference between what a person says and what he means. The effective listener is able to pick up those differences. In selling a product it is very important to know the reasons why the person does not want to buy—which isn't always the reason given. Lay ministers also should have training in effective listening. To be able to minister we must be able first to hear the calls for help. In fact, all of us could profit from some training in effective listening. Often when another person is speaking to us we are mentally composing a reply. We end up talking past each other and missing so much of what the other is trying to communicate. When someone wants to share a personal problem, he usually does not come right out with it. He will provide hints which, if picked up and developed by the listener, will open the way to discussion of the problem. So if a layperson is to minister to the needs of others, he must be a skillful listener.

Here again the church can provide support for laypersons. What's wrong with a Christian education program which offers a course in effective listening? In my twenty-five years of association with the church I have never once heard of a congregation or church agency offering people a course in how to listen. I have heard scores of sermons in which the faithful were charged to be the people of God in society. It apparently has never occured to the leaders of the church that the faithful could be more effective people of God in society if they were given some help in such a fundamental thing as the skill of listening.

Techniques for effective listening can easily be taught at the congregational level. One or two laypeople can be trained to conduct classes on how to listen. With the help of prepared materials and tape recorders, local laity can assist many of their fellow Christians to develop their skills in effective listening. A valuable by-product might be better communications between parents and children in our homes.

The second requirement of an aid man ministry is that the laypeople have enough training to be able to determine the nature and extent of a problem. Just as the combat medic had to be trained to recognize an injury that required professional help, so must the lay minister be able to perceive situations for which professional assistance is needed. Inability to determine the nature of a problem and lack of knowledge about how to help are the two greatest barriers today in keeping people from helping each other.

Several years ago a young woman, Kitty Genovese, was brutally killed on a New York street corner while some forty of her neighbors watched in silence from behind closed windows and locked doors. The incident has frequently been cited as a classic example of the indifference of people today. It became fertile ground for studies by psychologists.

The inital reaction which researchers got as they interviewed the neighbors of Kitty Genovese was that they didn't want to get involved. Why? Were they afraid? Yes, many were. Why? Why should they be afraid to call the police? As the questioning and probing continued, additional data began to appear.

The researchers were surprised to discover that a number of the neighbors of Kitty Genovese did not realize she was being attacked. Some said they thought it was a family fight on the street corner. In short, a number of the people were unable to diagnose the severity of the problem.

It was also learned that a larger group of the neighbors had never before been involved in crisis intervention and were generally convinced that any assistance they might provide would be dangerous to themselves. While this group recognized the problem, they had no experience or training in ways to assist without subjecting themselves to undue risks.

Similar types of studies have revealed that when a large group of people witness someone in distress, there is less likelihood of anyone providing help than if only one or two witnesses are at hand. The reason cited for this unusual behavior is that since most people feel totally inexperienced in helping in a crisis, they assume that in a large crowd there *must* be others who are more capable of helping than they. Therefore everyone holds back.

Another finding was that almost always a person who had previous training in first aid would respond to a call for help more readily than a person who never had such training. Such a conclusion is not surprising. First aid training does give people a measure of confidence that they will be able to diagnose certain kinds of problems and provide some degree of help.

If first aid training has given people confidence in responding to calls for help, why don't the church educational programs include courses in first aid for everyone? Many times the voice from the pulpit calls us to be our brother's keeper. Why does it stop with the rhetoric? Why aren't laypeople equipped in the techniques of being our brother's keepers?

Of course, much more than first aid training is needed to equip lay ministers to detect the injuries among their fellowmen. Many of us are totally inept in determining the signs of drug addiction, of alcoholism, and of various types of mental illness. It's surprising how many people are unable to distinguish between a spastic and a drunk.

The downtown church we belonged to several years ago was frequently visited by vagrants looking for a handout. A number of us tried to deal with these people as best we knew how. One Sunday a well-dressed stranger showed up in our church with a sad tale of troubles. My wife and I took him home for dinner and spent the better part of the day with him. We thought we had a good reading on his situation, so we offered him food and some money to help him through the next few days until we could get him to professional help. What we didn't know was that he was an alcoholic. He spent every cent we gave him on one large blast, and within two days he was dead! It was then that our church council realized how much we all needed some training in relating to derelicts. We called in experts—psycholgists, the police, representatives of Alcoholics Anonymous, and members of agencies who work with derelicts. Most of the leadership of the congregation attended the courses. But it took a tragedy to show us that we needed to be equipped if we want to minister to others.

There are many types of courses that can be offered to laypeople to help them understand or detect the problems of people they meet. Few people have had exposure to the subject of behavioral psychology. Some of us would benefit by having a psychologist spend some time with us on the basics of why people act the way they do, and how to tell the difference between behavioral patterns that can be helped by friends and those that need professional help.

A course in basic sociology would help many laypersons understand the types of pressures which surround poor people, or the types of living patterns associated with the cultures of various minority groups in our country.

I have found that many laypeople respond in a very positive manner to training in Transactional Analysis. While many professionals seem to take delight in criticizing TA, the fact remains that it has provided many people with a common vocabulary and a basic understanding for evaluating the communications they have with others. I think TA is a valuable tool for helping laypeople in their efforts to detect problems.

Many professionals, I am sure, will recoil at the thought of laypeople trying to "diagnose" other people's problems. I prefer to use the world "detect." Diagnosis implies a careful study by trained professionals; it is the task of those who are especially trained in various areas of study. But to detect is to discover, and laypeople should be equipped to discover problems at an early stage, with a view to dealing with them before they become worse.

When the combat medic detected an injury which was severe,

he immediately took steps to get the wounded to professional help. So too with the lay minister who serves in the role of aid man. His training must include a thorough familiarization with the professional resources available in the community. What are the resources available for dealing with drug problems, alcoholism, emotional problems, marriage problems, and medical problems? The lay minister must know where they are and how to reach them.

A third requirement is that the aid man know how to give direct aid himself where that is appropriate. Just as the combat medic is able to take care of those minor injuries not requiring professional attention, so too can the layperson provide a valuable ministry in dealing with the small hurts of life.

In order to do this one needs to become skilled in listening, and in asking questions in a nonjudgmental way. People should make their own decisions but a skillful lay minister can help the process along.

Many of us in middle age have all kinds of experiences we can share which will enable others to make their decisions better. We have lived on budgets, bought homes and cars, raised children, gone through illnesses and losses, moved, and done all the other things which go into living. The sharing of our *successes and failures* offers others additional data upon which to make their decisions, and a sense of human solidarity in approaching the issues. So there are times when the sharing of our own experiences can be a form of ministry.

For some laypeople there is even the possibility of doing some counseling. Why is the pastor the only one considered when family counseling is needed? There are often laypeople in the congregation who, by virtue of their personal experiences, may be potentially better counselors in certain areas. Who knows better what it is like to lose a husband when the children are young than a woman who has gone through it? Who can better help another cope with a crippling injury than one who has personally

experienced the same injury? A middle-aged couple who have had
a highly successful marriage and raised fine children have the
potential for being excellent family counselors. In a similar
manner laypeople can specialize in counseling on financial
matters, vocational situations, and preparation for retirement.

But again, the laypeople need to be equipped. Building upon
the experiences they have had in life, such lay ministers do need
training in the techniques of counseling. Quite possibly this is a
type of training that is best accomplished at a college or
seminary. Here the organized church can assist by seeing to it that
courses especially designed for equipping laypersons to counsel
are available at such schools of higher learning. This is one of
several areas of lay ministry where the requirements for further
education could indirectly assist colleges and seminaries with
their own financial problems. The cost for such education could
either be borne by the individual or by his supporting group, be it
a congregation or an unofficial Christian community.

The final requirement of the medical aid man was to be as
supportive as possible in his attitude as he assisted the wounded.
The lay minister is called to provide the same type of support.
Laypersons in their ministry to others will not be Pollyannas in
their disposition; rather they will have the inner confidence which
comes when they recognize that it is not they alone who minister,
but the risen Christ who is ministering through them. Through
their ministry they will share the virtues of faith, hope, and love.

Such is the style of the aid man ministry. It is not for all
laypersons by any means. But society has the need for such a
ministry, and there are many laypeople with the life experiences
to enable them to develop potentially effective ministries in this
area.

What is needed is the recognition of the validity of the aid man
style of ministry, the identification of gifts, the development of
skills, and the organization of the support groups to whom the
lay ministers can relate. The church can help in most of these
tasks.

6.

THE MINISTRY
OF
WORDS

Allan was a supervisor in one of the offices where I served as an assistant district sales manager. He was a devout, churchgoing man who saw a calling to relate his faith to his life. He had direct supervision of about twenty people, but because of his age and experience he felt very comfortable in his relationship to the other thirty people in the office, including his own supervisors.

Allan had a small, glass-enclosed office consisting of a desk, a bookcase, and three chairs. On his desk was a Bible. Whenever one of Allan's people had a problem of which he was aware, it became Allan's problem also. He would generally call the troubled person into his office, close the door, open the Bible and begin reading from it. Allan was convinced that all the solutions to the problems of our day could be found by locating an appropriate scripture passage. After reading that part of the Bible which he felt applied to the particular situation, Allan would frequently begin praying for the subordinate who was having the problem. He maintained a continuing interest in each worker's problems, and more than one person was invited back into his glass-enclosed office where, in full view of all, there were more Bible readings and prayers offered.

Allan was always ready to interpret the events of the day in terms of the scriptures to anyone in the office who seemed the least bit interested. The Cuban missle crisis, the assassination of President Kennedy, California earthquakes, and eastern hurricanes all could be understood if one only knew where to go in the Bible.

He was a conscientious and sincere man who loved and really cared about people. Because of this, very few things were said or done in that office which hurt Allan. And yet, behind his back, Allan was the subject of much joking. Whenever a personal problem arose, the standard advice surfaced: "For God's sake, don't tell Allan about it!"

As an assistant manager I had a supervisory responsibility for all the people in that office with the exception of my boss. Like Allan, I felt a calling to somehow relate my faith to the life situations in that office.

My private office was larger and more secluded than Allan's. No one could see when I was counseling with someone. There was no Bible on my desk. The closest I came to religious symbolism in my office was the dove of peace on the bookends our children had once given me as a present.

My style was different from Allan's. As a supervisor I was concerned about the ethics of injecting myself into the personal problems of one of our people without an invitation. Naturally, I could initiate discussions regarding job performance or commercial problems, but I felt it was violating the privacy of an individual to initiate a discussion involving personal problems not directly related to the job. Instead I tried hard to maintain an openness which would enable people to feel free to share personal problems with me if they wanted to. I have not been a naturally open person; it continues to be a talent I try to develop. There were not many who felt comfortable enough with me to share their personal problems with me. For those few who did seek my help, I tried to be nonjudgmental, yet helpful and supporting. It was never easy.

Although my motives for a ministry of counseling were based on my Christian faith, and although my personal ability to find meaning in life clearly related to my religious beliefs, I was seldom able to bring much of a theological dimension into my efforts to help others in our office. Not once did I feel comfortable in suggesting joint prayer. My prayers for the individual were always offered in private either before or after the counseling session.

I'm sure Allan's ministry of counseling and biblical interpretation involved twenty times as many occasions of sharing the faith as mine did. Knowing how everyone dismissed Allan's efforts as a slight eccentricity which was tolerated in kindness, I kept telling myself that my style of ministry was truly more helpful and effective even if it was less frequently called into play. I convinced myself of that, and, as I look back some ten years later, I still believe it to be true.

And yet I have always been troubled about something. I am convinced that if someone in that office had run a contest in which everyone had to rate everyone else as to whether he or she was a Christian, Allan's name would have been at the top of the list, and mine would have been somewhere down below.

Why should I be troubled by that fact? Was it because I wanted people in that office to recognize me as a "better" Christian than Allan? No, because I truly do not believe such judgments are humanly possible, nor is my acceptance in God's eyes based on any such ratings. What troubled me was the obvious fact that although my faith called me into a caring ministry for people, and although my faith was indeed an integral part of my very being, it was not that apparent to other people. Could it be that I was not committed enough to my faith to have the courage to share it with others? I don't think that was the reason. I feel strongly convinced about where I stand in my faith, and in other areas of life I have not been afraid of any ridicule or criticism by others. No, it was simply that I was not able to translate the teachings and language of my "church" world into the thought patterns and vernacular of the "real life" world.

I can recall many occasions when, in a group of Christians, the question came up as to what was the difference between a humanitarian act and a Christian act. "As long as the hungry are fed, does it matter whether the food was given by a Christian or a humanitarian?" I can hear someone ask. Another person will add, "Are we supposed to include a 'commercial' with our Christian deeds?" For many the very idea of a Christian ministering to someone's needs and then trying to proselytize is repugnant. It seems crassly manipulative. Indeed, if our motive for serving the needs of others is to provide a means of bringing more people into the membership of our faith, then we'd better reexamine the entire fabric of our Christian lives.

In a way, the humanitarian has it easy. For every good work he does, he can claim the credit. He alone is the instigator of every caring action which he extends to others. It is not so with me. I'd be a lousy humanitarian. I've got too much ego. Too often I'm so centered in myself that I can't focus on the needs of others. And so whenever I minister to the needs of others, I know it's not because of my basic nature. I know that God has been working in my life for years and he has been changing me into an outward-looking, caring person. I honestly cannot claim credit for my acts of ministry. Whatever I do in life today is because God has opened me up enough to let the living Christ serve others through me. I'm still quite successful at catering to my own ego, and taking a selfish position on many things. But to the extent that I do let Christ work through me, I must acknowledge that the credit belongs to him and not to me. That's the difference between a humanitarian act and a Christian act. And if that is true, then it does seem that there are occasions when, in complete ministry to another, we must verbalize that fact.

It is one thing to bring the thirsty person a drink of cool water; it is quite another thing to bring him cool water *and* tell him where he can get more. There are times when the ministry we provide is not complete unless it includes an explanation of its source. Depending upon the situation, the ministry of the laity may involve a spoken witness of the faith, an act of service, or both.

Admittedly, not all Christian people see it this way. There are those who say that the contemporary Christian's witness to his faith must be based solely on his style of life and the way he serves his fellowman. This viewpoint maintains that we cannot talk someone into our faith—it is only God who initiates the encounter with man. They say that those who try to convert others by reciting scripture verses or arguing concepts are really trying to manipulate people, that it is only by the example of the life we lead that we are able to offer a faith to others.

At the other end of the scale are those Christians who feel called to witness to others solely through the spoken word. They will hand out literature in shopping malls and airports. They will eagerly seek out opportunities to engage others in conversation about their faith. Some will canvass neighborhoods, ringing doorbells and asking to be invited in to discuss the basics of their faith. They maintain that humanists and atheists do good work also, and no man is so perfect in his deeds that it is obvious to others that his source of ministry springs from his Christian faith.

Both viewpoints support their position by citing the examples of Jesus. And that, in itself, says something.

There are many instances in the New Testament where Jesus ministered to the needs of people without any recorded message of why he was doing it. There are even some encounters where he instructed others *not* to tell about him. The healing of the leper in the eighth chapter of Matthew is such an example. It is true that a strong argument can be made that the crowds were attracted to Jesus more by what he did than by what he said.

Yet it is equally true that Jesus frequently used the occasions of his ministering to others to tell them about the kingdom of God. There are even instances where Jesus used the act of healing to reinforce a point of his teaching. Such an example can be found in the twelfth chapter of Matthew when Jesus heals the man with a crippled hand on the Sabbath to reinforce his teaching that the law does allow helping others on the holy day.

It would seem, therefore, that Jesus proclaimed the faith to others both by what he did and by what he said. Indeed, when he sent others out in his name, he instructed them to do both. When he sent the Twelve out on a mission he said, "Go and preach 'The Kingdom of Heaven is near'! Heal the sick, raise the dead, make the lepers clean, drive out demons" (Matt. 10:7).

Those engaged in lay ministries today should strive for the same style of proclaiming the faith. There are times when the ministry calls solely for meeting specific needs. There are times when the ministry calls for a sharing of the faith through the spoken word. And there are times when the two go hand in hand. It is for the lay minister to decide in any given situation which means of communication truly express the will of God at that time.

Neither Allan nor I were effective ministers. Allan's approach to communicating the faith was too simplistic, and somewhat insensitive. His efforts to lift out Bible passages as solutions to all types of personal problems and world situations insulted the intelligence of almost everyone. His style of praying with someone in that fishbowl of an office keenly embarrassed many of those who were involved.

My approach was not simplistic. Unfortunately, neither was it complete. Although some of the people I ministered to had simple problems, a number of the others revealed problems which suggested the lack of any spiritual foundation in their lives. While I did not believe quoting Bible verses was the effective entry point for discussing spiritual values in life, I was hard pressed to find a good key. There were times when I asked if the person, or his family, attended church. No matter which way the answer came back, I would usually follow up with some expressions of what churchgoing meant in my life. And yet I felt uncomfortable with that approach. I knew very well that the act of sitting through a church service was not going to solve personal problems, and the chances were that it would not necessarily even bring a spiritual dimension into a person's life. Those who live in a continuing relationship with God know that the faith is nurtured by many more events than worship alone. And so I spent many years of frustration in a ministry which seemed very unbalanced. There were so many obvious ways to minister to others in deeds; the ministry of words was lacking.

In general there are three ways in which laypersons minister to others through their spoken word. First, we minister by the way we express our own values, our outlook on life, our style of life. Second, we minister by the way we express our viewpoint on issues of the day. And finally, we minister when we explain the teachings of our faith. Let's look at each of these in some detail.

No one can challenge the statement that we live in a time of turmoil and uncertainty. Where does one begin with the listing of the problems facing all of us on this finite piece of real estate we call earth? On a global scale we are struggling with the very real concern of overpopulation and the resultant problem of hunger. The "have-not" nations are fiercely determined to gain their fair share of the world's resources, and their efforts are punctuated with nationalistic sabre rattling, economic power plays, and international blackmail. In our own country we have gone through about fifteen years of social, economic, and political changes unlike any period in our history. The civil rights movement, the Vietnam War, the counterculture movement, the women's liberation movement, the Watergate scandal, the deterioration of our cities, the drug problem, the increasing crime rates, pollution, recession, inflation, the virtual financial collapse of our railroads and major cities—the list can go on. For the first time in history a president and a vice-president of our country resigned in dishonor. The basic building block of our society, the family, is threatened with collapse. Few people trust our institutions; fewer trust our leaders. We have had a variety of political assassinations and attempted assassinations. All our moral and religious values have been sharply questioned. Advances in medicine prolong life, but we don't know what to "do" with the elderly. People are angry about welfare programs, dishonesty in government, strikes by civil servants, "pampering" of criminals, busing, rising taxes, and falling incomes. Despair and pessimism grow; confidence and hope fade. Our heroes are dead.

Fifteen years ago the doomsayers were a minority; today the optimist is an incredibly rare bird. People are desperate for assurance, hungry for hope.

The Christian has no pat solution to any of the myriad of problems we face as a people. Nor can we escape them. But I must attest to the observation that those friends of mine who are committed to the faith are certainly better able to cope with the problems. The Christian faith offers meaning for being, purpose for life, and hope for the future. For those of us who see who we are with respect to our Creator, and who are assured of the constant love of that Creator, there is a focus to the whole of life which enables us to have strength and hope when others are in despair.

The apostle Paul expressed it well in his letter to the church at Rome: "What can separate us from the love of Christ? Can affliction or hardship? Can persecution, hunger, nakedness, peril, or the sword?" And then he concludes with that bold statement of faith, "For I am convinced that there is nothing in death or life, in the realm of spirits or superhuman powers, in the world as it is or the world as it shall be, in the forces of the universe, in heights or depths—nothing in all creation that can separate us from the love of God in Christ Jesus our Lord" (Rom. 8:35; NEB).

That's solid. That's a statement every committed Christian can make. That's a truth that endures even as the layers of confidence peel off our cherished institutions of strength. The more everything else in life seems to weaken, the more obvious becomes the truth of that firm relationship to our Creator.

How does this assurance of the Christian's relationship to God and all of creation translate into words for laypeople? When laypeople are out there in the real world, using words like hope, assurance, confidence, joy, satisfaction, purpose, meaning, love, and caring, they are betraying a style of life which is significantly different from that of people who are not in touch with their God. We should be aware of the positive words in our vocabulary and not be shy about using them. They can convey more about us then we would expect.

We've come through a period when the word *peace* carried with it all sorts of significance. The antiwar movement used it so much that for a few years it was virtually impossible to utter the word without betraying where you stood on the matter of the Vietnam War. I very well remember the first Christmas season the single word *peace* began appearing on holiday greeting cards. Our family sent such greeting cards out, and it was clear to all where we stood on the Southeast Asia issue.

In a similar manner it seems to me that select and even extensive use of the word *hope,* or *joy*—or any word which expresses our confidence in who we are and why we are here— can become the start of a ministry of words. The Christian is not a Pollyanna, but in a world where many are in despair he does have reason to hope.

Can our ministry of words begin with such a simple thing as a studied use of those words which describe our personal outlook on life? It can if we keep in mind the parable of the sower.

The synoptic Gospels relate the parable of the man who went out to sow. "As he scattered the seed in the field, some of it fell along the path, and the birds came and ate it up. Some of it fell on rocky ground, where there was little soil. . . Some of the seed fell among thorns, which grew up and choked the plants. . . . But some seeds fell in good soil, and the plants sprouted, grew, and bore grain." In explaining the parable, Jesus says, "The sower sows God's message." He then explains how the message may fall along the path, or on rocky ground, or among the thorns and it dies.

But that seed which falls in good soil is like the people who "hear the message, accept it, and bear fruit" (Mark 4:14; TEV).

Again, in the parable of the mustard seed, Jesus says the kingdom of God is like the smallest seed in the world. "A man takes it and, sows it in his field, and when it grows up it is the biggest of all plants" (Matt. 13:31; TEV).

The words and expressions we use in daily conversation which reveal our outlook on life can indeed be very small seeds. But they are seeds. Within them lie the potential to develop a ministry of words into a large tree of communicating the faith. The parable of the sower does not suggest that the one who scatters the seed also has the power to develop the plant. No, the plant is developed by a power that comes from elsewhere.

It is God's initiative and not man's which causes the seed of God's message to develop within a human being. We, as lay ministers, are called to scatter the seed and watch for those instances when it falls on fertile ground so that as God develops it we can be supportive with feeding and cultivation.

The key code words we use may be seeds we can scatter. The manner in which we express our viewpoint on various matters can also be seeds which reveal our lifestyle.

In the business circles in which I move, I frequently come in contact with people who are extremely materialistic. Everything has a price. There is a frantic compulsion to outdo all one's friends in having the best or the most of everything there is. And, without exception, the people obsessed with materialism are unhappy. They never have enough. So how do we minister to such people through our words? Do we take a deep breath and bravely quote 1 Timothy 6:10, "The love of money is the root of all evil," and follow it up with a lecture? Hardly. We drop seeds.

One of the antimaterialism seeds I frequently drop is a kind of tirade against the fashion industry which is forever trying to change styles and thereby pressure all of us to buy new clothing when what we have is perfectly usable. Or I may criticize Detroit for trying to con me into buying a new car just because the style changes, not because my old one is worn out. Materialistic people don't like to think they're being taken, and sometimes dropping the right seed will cause them to engage in a serious conversation regarding the whole business of the use of money.

Another antimaterialism seed I drop relates to what I've learned watching our children grow up. The two older ones are now married, and were a part of the counterculture movement of the '60s. I've seen firsthand how the youth of today can find happiness totally apart from materialistic obsession. I'm not saying all our youth are happy; many are not. But those who are happy generally are enjoying a lifestyle unencumbered by excessive cares about material needs. Since it is conventional to let people talk about their children, I usually can talk freely about the values our children hold regarding materialism. And to link happiness with a rejection of materialism blows the minds of many highly materialistic people. Sometimes these seeds open the way for in-depth discussions about the real values in life.

Another characteristic of the type of people I frequently encounter in business is that they often tend to be judgmental. "All people on welfare are lazy" is a frequent comment I hear. "We should put all criminals behind bars for a long time—then we'd reduce crime," is another. Or "Every politician in Washington is crooked." Unfortunately, people tend to reinforce each other with such statements and the result is that people are unjustly condemned.

How does the Christian layperson minister to those who are terribly judgmental about others? Do we gulp and piously quote Matthew 7:1, "Judge not that you be not judged"? I'd strike out on doing that.

But again, we can drop seeds. When people become judgmental, I frequently play the game, "I wonder what it's like." "I wonder what it's like to be retired with no pension and have to go on welfare?" I ask. "I wonder what it's like to be in prison for a year?" "I wonder what it's like to be a lawmaker in Washington with so many different viewpoints coming from my constituents?"

Sometimes those seeds strike fertile ground, and people begin imagining what it *is* like. And from such beginnings come discussions which may go into greater depth regarding understanding and justice. The game of "I wonder what it's like" doesn't always work, but there have been times when I've been absolutely fascinated to see how a judgmental person can get into the role of a person he was criticizing and end up defending that person's actions.

There are many people in the world who are frightened. We run across people every day who are afraid to try a new food, afraid to fly in an airplane, afraid of "what people might say," afraid to speak up for their rights. How many people go through life with so many worries and fears that they really never know what it is like to be a free person? They are prisoners of their own anxieties.

The Christian life is not one given to great fears. This is not suggest that a Christian is careless, indifferent to danger, and irresponsible. Instead he is an open person who can see himself in the context of a total situation. He has positive feelings about himself and others because he knows that God loves and accepts him. So while he tries to use good judgment as he faces life situations, he is not afraid of failure, not obsessed with securing the approval of others, and not overly concerned about the future or the unknown.

How does a ministry of words convey this freedom and openness of the Christian to his brothers and sisters who are prisoners of their own anxieties? Do we quote "You shall know the truth, and the truth will set you free" (John 8:32; NEB)? Or "Consider the lilies" (Matt. 6:25)? I don't think it would be effective.

Perhaps in this type of communicating of the faith, we resort to a bit of "show and tell." Perhaps we weave into our normal conversations some of those things we have done in life which have resulted from Christian growth—our breaking out of a prison of self-centeredness and anxiety.

"I used to hate to rock the boat, but now my family calls me the 'mad letter writer'."

"In the past thirty years I have become more liberal in my viewpoint on many things."

"I used to be a very shy person, but now I really enjoy meeting strangers."

"Our children have had a big effect in changing my thoughts about a lot of things."

"If anyone would have told me thirty years ago that I'd be marching in the streets of Washington, D.C., in protest against our government, I would have said they were crazy."

"I've really grown to like variety in foods (or travel, or worship forms)."

All these statements—which I can honestly make—relate to change in my life. They start from where the other person may now be and go on to describe a position where I now am. Generally people are interested in following up on such statements. They want to know more. They want to know why. And from such openers sometimes comes a fruitful conversation which works its way back to basic religious concepts.

To be a Christian is to grow. Therefore all of us must be able to point to areas of our life which have changed because of our Christian growth. We forget that others may sometimes assume that we have always been open, hopeful, liberated personalities. To relate examples in our own lives wherein we changed from needless anxiety to a freer spirit enables others to identify with us better and invites them to probe deeper into what makes us tick.

The use of hope-filled "code words" and the dropping of seeds which reveal our lifestyle are, of course, merely means of encouraging greater inquiry on the part of others. It seems to me that we have to start where the other person presently is. Once the other person can identify with us, then we can bring the conversation along towards a greater sharing of our faith. But when we start by lecturing, or quoting Bible verses, or being critical, the other person is not going to want to follow any course of conversation simply because he is not with us.

The openers I have used as examples do not always work. They are ones I've had to develop on my own, by trial and error. It's had to be that way since never, in my long association with the church, have I ever been part of a program in which laypeople are helped to develop means of initiating discussions about the faith. Most evangelism programs I've been associated with simply focus on sending out laypeople to ring doorbells and invite people to their church. While it does take courage for laypeople to do this, I have always had the feeling that I was not making an authentic statement of my faith when the totality of my message was to invite a person to join my church.

When a seed does fall on fertile ground and begin to develop, the lay minister should be prepared to encourage God's growth through feeding, watering, and cultivating. As the seed of faith begins to sprout within a person, he may want to discuss some important issues in his life with a lay minister. When this phase of growth begins, the layperson must be able to bring his own theological perspectives into play.

As I look back over twenty-five years of active involvement in the institutional church, it is discouraging to note how little of contemporary theological thought was ever presented to the laity. Few indeed are the laity who can say that their church introduced them to the current theological perspectives which were appearing within ecclesiastical enclaves. Quite the contrary. Most laypeople who are aware of the theological perspectives presented in such books as *Honest to God, Situation Ethics, Secular City,* and *A Theology of Hope* received their introductions through their local bookstore and not through their church. Whoever heard of Teilhard de Chardin or even Bonhoeffer being introduced into the ongoing life of a congregation?

In fact, it seems that more often than not, current theological writings which attract attention at bookstores are disparaged from the pulpit without the laity ever hearing both sides of the issue. It is bad enough that the laity must turn to their bookstores to learn of new theological writings, but it is almost incredible to see the way in which the institutional church quickly forms the wagon train into a circle to defend against "popularized theology." The laity are treated like intellectual babies—a fact which partially explains why many thinking people have parted company with their church.

A few years ago I read the book *I'm OK, You're OK* by Thomas Harris. It had immediate appeal for me because it put into simple terms the many behavioral patterns of people. Our Christian community spent time studying it, and ever since we have had a common language base for communicating behavior concepts to each other. Our family, including all our children, have found the Parent-Child-Adult concepts ideal in dealing with crossed communications within our homes. I also began to see that the book's popularity offered a new means for communicating truths of our faith to others through the spoken word. In recent years I've used the language of *I'm OK, You're OK* as an entry point for discussing religion with those who are floundering spiritually. In talking about the importance of having an "O.K." feeling about yourself, it is a short step to a sharing of the truth that God accepts us as being O.K. people even though we often fail. Harris has convincingly demonstrated that the truly O.K. person also has O.K. feelings about others. So, too, we can say that when we are in an O.K. relationship with God, we accept others as being O.K. even though they too are not perfect. It seems to me that this basic relationship we have with God and with others is really the cornerstone of our faith. Jesus certainly preached and lived the O.K. relationship with his Father and with others. I'm grateful to Dr. Harris for this book. It has enabled me to find a reasonable entry point for bringing the religious dimension into some situations.

I can understand why psychologists scoff at the book. It is too simplistic, they say. I know that is so. The behavior of human beings cannot be so easily catalogued. But for the purposes of nonprofessional communication, it has been ideal. What I cannot understand is why so many clergymen discard the book so lightly.

They seem to fall in step with the professional psychologists and echo the complaint that the high science of describing human behavior is much more complex. What they seem to have missed is the obvious opportunity to translate the church theological language into words well recognized and understood by most laypeople today. The term "justification by faith through grace alone" is still bounced around within the walls of our churches, but it means nothing out there on Main Street, U.S.A. But if I say to someone, "God's gift to you is to stamp you O.K. and if you believe that it's true, it will be true," he understands a basic concept of our faith. He may not accept the idea, but at least he understands it. Unfortunately quite a few clergy prefer to stick with the traditional theological language of the church, and leave it up to the laypeople to try to figure out how to translate these ideas to others in the "real world." Terms like *salvation, atonement,* and *sanctification* simply are meaningless to those outside the church. No wonder we laypeople have difficulty communicating the faith!

One keeps coming back to the question, Why? Why doesn't the church encourage laypeople to become acquainted with contemporary theological thought? Why does the church react to soaring bookstand sales of current theological insights with knee-jerk condemnation from the pulpits? Why does the church depreciate those literary works which provide a helpful means for laity to relate faith to life?

Those questions of *why* lead into more penetrating questions. Just what *is* the church doing today in the area of theology? Where is new theological thought being encouraged? How much should parish pastors be expected to be able to deliver in new theological concepts?

Elton Trueblood says, "One of the most surprising weaknesses of the Christian ministry in the recent past has been the neglect of rigorous theology." In his book *Can Man Hope to be Human?* Wallace Fisher says, "The laity's outspoken criticism or quiet rejection of the church's teachings (content, language, logic) must be heard and considered, challenged, and affirmed. Laymen who think for themselves will not accept irrelevant dogmas. They will not respond to shallow homilies on religion. They will not get involved in the community of faith through evangelistic programs designed to 'con' newcomers into joining the local congregation."

There may be arguments about whether or not the church belongs in the business of social welfare programs, or housing, or national politics. There can be no argument, however, about the fact that the church *does* belong in the theology business!

As a layperson who struggles with the relationship of my faith to my life, I say that the church has badly neglected that one area of our culture that is assuredly its domain—theology.

It is true that there are a number of religious publications in America which regularly publish articles and perspectives on current theological thought. But they are circulated solely for the "in" group of professionals, and, very frankly, they generally are wordy and frightfully dull. The temptation to debate on how many angels can dance on the head of a pin apparently is ever with the professional religious thinker.

Not only should our churches recognize that many laypersons are interested in current theological trends in our world, they should also acknowledge that a twenty-minute sermon, delivered once a week, to an audience of several hundred people runs counter to all basic educational principles. What is needed is for the laity to have small-group dialogue with a theologian on a subject which *they* select. For too long adult educational materials in our churches have been answering questions which no one was really asking. Instead of professionals determining what should be the content of adult educational materials, let's begin a style wherein the layperson comes to his church knowing that there will be a dialogue on those matters in his life for which he is searching for theological perspectives.

At some time or another, all Christian laypeople are faced with the opportunity to minister to others through the spoken word. It is important that our words be honest and credible. If in our everyday lives we do not normally verbalize ideas or philosophize with others, we would be out of character to try to express deep theological concepts. On the other hand, the person who enjoys discussing political, scientific, economic, or social ideologies should certainly consider that the development of his talent can lead to a style of lay ministry. For such a person the church must provide support. These lay ministers must be introduced to contemporary theological thought, must have frequent contacts with competent professionals in theology, and should have many opportunities for participation in educational programs at the colleges and seminaries of the church. While some seminaries have been offering programs to laypersons, they have tended to be simplified versions of the courses presented to theological students. The real leap forward for seminaries will come when they begin to deliver courses which help the layperson to bridge the gap between historic doctrines of the faith and swiftly changing contemporary events. The day could come when our seminaries have a larger population of laypersons tied into various types of educational programs than they have prospective clergy. When that day comes, the quality of education of young clergy will be significantly improved also.

If we can honestly say that our faith has brought joy, peace, hope, and love into our lives, then we should be conscious of the opportunity to share these blessings with others through the spoken word. If we can honestly say that our faith has changed our lives and freed us from anxiety, then we should be alert to the possibilities of helping another find what we have found through our firsthand reporting.

Words and deeds—both channels reveal to others something about ourselves. Both channels provide opportunities to minister to others in need. The ministry of laity in the world today calls for skills in both.

7.

THE MINISTRY
OF
ETHICS

Doug was a salesman, a hard worker and very loyal to the company. He was sincere in everything he did. But he was not bright. He did not have the intellectual capacity to handle his assignment properly. It became a management responsibility of mine to help deal with the problem.

A review of his personnel record suggested that from the very beginning there had been a series of management errors. Doug's academic record alone should have cautioned any interviewer against hiring him for the type of job he was seeking. Quite possibly his eagerness or sincerity impressed those who decided to employ him. Whatever the reason, a mistake was made in hiring Doug in the first place.

From there on, the management mistakes continued. Because he was a willing worker, and dedicated to the company, other managers tried to work around his intellectual weakness by switching him to other assignments within the department. Through the years he received salary increases which were more rewards for loyalty and hard work than for performance. His file revealed that a series of well-meaning managers had tried to solve the problem by searching for "the right spot for Doug." But errors continued to be made.

Looking at the situation in retrospect, one could easily conclude that Doug never should have been hired for the job in the first place. Once the initial mistake was made, it should have been corrected while he was still young enough to find another career opportunity.

Doug was now forty-five years old. He had invested twenty-two years of his life in our company. Based on merit and potential, he could never advance any farther in responsibility or salary. In short, he was at the end of his career at age forty-five. When most men with his age and experience are just reaching their career peaks, Doug was done. And it was not his fault. He had always done the best job of which he was capable. He was always willing to try something new. The fault had to lie with his employer who had made a series of mistakes.

How does a manager who tries to bring a Christian perspective into his work deal with such a situation? What is the just thing to do?

The interests of a number of people were involved in this problem. First, there was Doug. With his limited amount of talent he was too old to begin a new career at age forty-five. What would happen to him as a person, and to his family, if he were to be fired or demoted? What would happen to his self-esteem? Is it fair that he should pay for earlier management errors?

Then there were Doug's co-workers. Some of them had helped to carry Doug's load. All of them recognized that management was not facing up to the fact of Doug's poor performance. Doug was holding down a position into which a more qualified person could move and do a better job. Was it fair to penalize his co-workers because management had made a mistake with Doug?

Next, there were the unseen workers in our steel mills, and our stockholders, whose livelihood depended upon the quality of our sales effort. To the extent that Doug's poor performance lost business for us, these people were indirectly hurt. Was it fair to them to have to take a penalty, however slight, because Doug was continued in the assignment he held?

Our decision was a compromise and, as is often the case in compromises, no one was completely satisfied. Doug was demoted in function but not in salary. His ego was bruised and it obviously hurt to take an assignment of lesser importance. However, in recognition of previous management errors, it was agreed that Doug should not get a pay cut. That was the company's contribution to the problem. Another, more able, employee in the office got Doug's assignment. While Doug's co-workers recognized that management had acted to correct a bad situation, there was a lingering feeling that Doug was not fired outright because of personal friendships he had with management. While the steelworkers and stockholders were now given the type of top sales effort to which they were entitled, now corporate resources disproportionate to his contribution were still going to Doug. And as a manager I knew we had sacrificed a bit of management integrity in doing what we did. In short, everyone involved had to pay something to arrive at our solution.

From time to time I will hear pastors talk about the ethical decisions Christian laymen must make in business. They list such matters as polluting the environment, product liability, engaging in illegal activities, producing materials for war, providing affirmative action in minority hiring, dealing with countries which practice discrimination. These are crucial ethical issues which must be faced by American business. But they are issues which tend to reflect the decisions of top management since they are issues of corporate policy. The proportion of Christian laypersons who participate in corporate policy making is very small. Unfortunately, many clergy are totally unaware of the types of ethical decisions which laypersons face within corporations today, decisions which are quite common and unrelated to corporate policy making.

Perhaps the largest area of ethical decision making for laypersons in corporations or other institutions involves the treatment of other people. There are thousands of Dougs in our society. There are thousands of lazy people, thousands of overly aggressive people, thousands of dishonest people, thousands of misfits, and thousands of disheartened people working within our economic system. Christian laypersons are there in the midst of the ethical decision making which must be faced as people-problems arise.

There are ethical problems involving honesty. While honesty is not the exclusive concern of the Christian, it is important that Christians be truthful in dealing with every day problems. On the one hand the laity will hear admonitions from the church that they should absolutely be honest in everything they do. On the other hand, they see occasional instances in which honesty is not the wisest, fairest, or most loving thing to practice.

Suppose you are a shipping clerk responsible for loading kegs of nails on outgoing trucks. You discover that on a previous day you made a mistake and shipped out an order for 505 kegs when there should have been only 500. The customer's bill will only be for 500 kegs, however. You know that to reclaim the five extra kegs will cost your employer more than the nails themselves are worth. Therefore, the best interests of your employer are served if you do not correct the error. Is this dishonest?

Suppose you are a salesman of heavy construction equipment. You are calling on the purchasing agent of a large company dressed in one of your newest suits. Suddenly your office contacts you to say that one of your company's best customers is having a problem with a piece of equipment on a big construction job. You are instructed to get there immediately, because the entire project is shut down. Since you don't have time to go home and change into working clothing, you arrive on the project in your new suit. You get the equipment operating again, but in the process your new suit is torn. In reporting the matter to your boss, you mentioned the loss of a new suit. The company has a policy of not paying for clothing damaged on field calls, since salesmen are expected to dress in work clothing when they plan such visits.

But under these circumstances, your boss suggests that you

"bury" the cost of your suit in your expense account. He says that it is only fair that the company pay you for your loss, and you agree. But the only way to achieve that result is for you to enter some false items on your expense account at the end of the month. Are you being honest?

You are a typist in a secretarial pool. Your company requires that all employees punch a time clock when they begin and end work. Those who punch in late are penalized in their pay, and excessive tardiness results in automatic dismissal. You have a friend who is a working mother. Because of occasional problems with her children in the morning she is sometimes late getting to work. She has asked you to punch her time card on those mornings when she misses the bus you usually travel on together. Although the company has a firm rule against punching the time clock of another, you do it anyway because your friend is one of the fastest typists in the office and always forgoes her coffee break on those days on which she is late. You know she needs the money and you know she gives your employer a full day's work, even when she is late. Is it dishonest for you to cover for her?

The church must recognize that the matter of ethics in business or society goes far beyond the broad, policy-making decisons made by a handful of top executives in any given institution. Granted that the Eli Blacks and others in high office need the concern and support of the church in the ethics of setting policy, but so do all the laypersons in lesser jobs who seek to do what is just and honest and loving in their daily work situations. How can such laypersons be supported?

During the time I was struggling with the problem of what to do about Doug, Judy and I were members of a small Christian support group of laypersons from our local congregation. Because the group had established a style of personal problem sharing and had demonstrated the ability to maintain confidentiality, I shared with them my concerns about Doug.

The support group was varied in its makeup. Of the fourteen

men and women in it, only one other member was a business manager. This fact forced me to describe the problem in full detail so that everyone could understand. In itself, a careful review of all the details was helpful in assuring me that nothing was overlooked. A number of my statements were challenged. One person did not agree that the stockholders' interests came into play at all. There were some antibusiness statements that we had to work through. Several people forced me to give greater thought to Doug's wife and children.

Throughout the one evening which was devoted to my problem, there was no suggestion that the group would ultimately make my decision for me. It was well recognized that it was my problem in my arena of Christian ministry and that I alone had to make the final decision as to where I stood. But the group helped my decision making greatly by asking unexpected questions, probing all the alternatives, and trying to integrate those Christian perspectives which would apply. At the end of the evening, during our period of prayer, various members of the support group prayed that I would be led to that decision which best expressed the will of God.

Readers of this book may take issue with the decision which was made. Some may feel it was too harsh on Doug; others may feel it was too soft. Nevertheless, I feel satisfied with the decision because of my support group. They forced me to face all the issues squarely, they helped assure me that a Christian concern was part of the decision, and they made it clear that their prayers were supportive in what was an agonizing struggle of a lay minister.

Over the years I have reported to the group from time to time on Doug's status. The group is still concerned and I am still held accountable to them to report on the situation. That is real support!

Our society is so fantastically complex today that it is very difficult to decide what is the most just, most loving position to take on many ethical issues. We need all the help we can get to make certain we are being honest with ourselves and to see how our Christian faith applies. Every layperson who wants to relate his faith to his everyday life should have access to a Christian support group, I am convinced.

From the Congress of the United States to groups of common laborers there are numerous Christian support groups which exist solely for the purpose of helping their members relate their faith to the activities of daily life. They are almost always lay organized and have lay leadership. If there are clergy in such groups their role is to function as observers or theological interpreters.

In 1963, The National Council of Churches published a book called *On-The-Job-Ethics* which reported on a pilot program involving six different occupational groups. Under the sponsorship of the Division of Christian Life and Work of the NCC, groups of bankers, building contractors, business executives, labor leaders, personnel people, and public relations people met for varying periods of time to examine the ethical problems they face and how their faith related to such problems.

Since I have been involved with the furnishing of steel products to the construction industry for twenty-five years, I was greatly interested in the report of the building contractors and associates. The construction industry is fertile ground for ethical discussions. For those not familiar with the American system of competitive bidding for construction projects, a brief explanation is necessary.

When a new building is to be constructed the owner (private company, individual, school board) hires an architect to draw up plans. When final designs have been completed, general contractors are invited to submit bids for construction. The bid represents the contractor's offer to construct the complete building for a stated amount of money, based on his own estimate of the material and labor costs involved. In order to prepare the bids, the general contractor must also secure bids from various material suppliers for such items as bricks, steel, cement, windows, and tile floors. Furthermore, since most general contractors cannot handle all the specialized phases of construction, they must secure subcontract bids from specialty contractors for such things as plumbing, electrical work, heating, and air conditioning.

On any given building contract there can be from three to ten or more general contractors preparing their own estimates and securing bids from scores of material suppliers and specialty subcontractors.

At an appointed time, the sealed bids of the contractors are received by the owner, and the one with the lowest bid is usually awarded the work. In other words, the building project is put into the hands of that contractor who has the least amount of money provided for doing the work. Moreover, since each bid is based on an estimate of the cost of doing the work, there is always the possibility that the successful bidder made an error in his estimate and is therefore destined to lose money on the project. What kind of commitment to quality of construction will a contractor have if he discovers he is about to lose money on the job? Will he cut corners? Will he try to furnish inferior materials?

The general contractors, in turn, want to make the most favorable deal they can in purchasing materials and awarding subcontracts to the specialists. Frequently one vendor is played off against the other in an effort to get them to reduce their prices. Some contractors operate on the gamble that they can make a profit on their job by successfully beating down the prices of their suppliers. Therefore even the successful suppliers start out with orders at marginal prices. How intent will they be upon furnishing quality materials and services? Many ethical questions can be raised about the tactics used in "shopping" for materials and services. Deception and outright dishonesty are commonplace.

If the architect has made an error in his designs, or if he is not clear in his intent, some contractors may intentionally offer a very low bid so that they can secure the work and then make a profit on the correcting of the architect's error or through litigation over interpretation of plans and specifications. It's hardly an ethical practice, but it is not uncommon.

When interest rates are high, the one who has money in his possession for any period of time can put it to work for himself. Some contractors have a reputation for withholding money from their suppliers or subcontractors for the slimmest of reasons. More than one small subcontractor has been driven to bankruptcy because a general contractor withheld payment for work done.

Finally, there is the matter of construction labor forces. The number of long-term employees on a contractor's payroll is usually a small percentage of the total number of workers he uses on a construction job. Many workers are hired out of union halls for certain types of work such as common labor, carpentry, cement finishing, and bricklaying. When they have completed their portion of the project, they leave the contractor's payroll, and begin looking for work at some other job. Without the long-term employer-employee relationship common to most businesses, there are frequently personnel problems and indifference to productivity. Each building trade has its own union—carpenters, masons, ironworkers, equipment operators—and each union negotiates its own contracts with the contractors. Strikes and jurisdictional disputes are commonplace.

This is the everyday environment of the building contractor. It is an arena in which deception, dishonesty, shoddy workmanship, and poor employee relationships are too often the accepted mode of operation.

How did the National Council of Churches project relate to the group of building contractors? The convener of the group, Robert C. Batchelder, wrote, "Apart from whether the church was able to contribute anything specific in the way of insight or practical guidance, the very fact that it was involved in such a series of discussions was probably of help in implying that what

happens in a man's work is of importance to God and in providing support and encouragement to those struggling to improve
the practices in the industry."

On the other hand, many of the participants were disappointed that the clergy-observer was unable to provide distinctly
"ethical" or "religious" solutions to their dilemmas. Batchelder
felt that this disappointment, while it may have represented
a naive expectation on the part of the contractors, also represented a failure of the church today: "The church does not know
how to speak the eternal truth of the gospel in a way that can be
understood and appropriated by modern industrialized man."

Most of the contractors and suppliers in the group were active
churchmen, serving on church governing bodies and committees,
and even as Sunday School teachers. They were well acquainted
with the teachings of their faith. Yet Batchelder noted, "When
the attempt was made to relate the central doctrines of the faith
to the issues we had been discussing, there was scarcely a sign of
recognition." The convener felt that his lack of skill in interpreting may have been at fault, but he also suggests that the church's
traditional phrases and ideas "have lost their power to move
man."

Batchelder concludes: "Surely the task of the clergy leader in
such a group as this must be to contribute to the conversation by
articulating the insights of the Christian faith in such a way that
they are both relevant to the issues under consideration and also
meaningful to those who hear. This means that one of the crucial
challenges confronting the church today is to rediscover within its
tradition those words and ideas and insights that will strike the
spark of response in twentieth-century industrialized men and
enable them to renew and reorder their lives and their work in
response to the gracious action of God."

The pilot project of the National Council of Churches provides
an excellent model of the way in which Christian laypersons in
allied occupations can come together in faith-work studies. In

this instance concerned Christian laypersons were brought together by the church to write an agenda of their mutual concerns
involving ethics and human relationships. A clergyman was provided whose function was to listen and to try to relate the theology of the faith to the real-life situations. When that day comes
that the style of the NCC pilot project can be multiplied by the
thousands across our country, then we will be well on the way
towards closing that faith-work gap which so obviously exists
today.

All of us have reason to be concerned about ethics in our
society. Lay ministers can serve society well by endeavoring to
introduce Christian values into the ethical issues of everyday life.
This can be done in two ways.

First, as they meet together in small groups, laypersons should
have the willingness to share with their fellow believers the types
of ethical problems they confront. A true support group, regard-
less of its basic objectives, will have the flexibility to alter its
agenda at any time in order to deal with personal needs of its
members. A prayer group, for example, should be free enough
to take time out to help a member sift through the Christian
implications of an ethical decision he is wrestling with. As illus-
trated in the story about Doug, significant help can come even
from a group which is not drawn from the same occupational
background. Diversity sometimes has the benefit of uncovering
perspectives which had been overlooked before. On the other
hand, occupational support groups, such as the building contractors who met in Detroit, are well enough acquainted with
the technical aspects of an ethical problem that they can insure
total honesty in the presentation of the situation. Furthermore,
occupational support groups sometimes have the potential for
helping a member to implement an action course which has been
decided upon.

Accountability is a unique feature of every good support
group. After a member shares his ethical dilemma with the group,

he is expected to arrive at his own decision and act on it. From time to time he will report back to the group on his progress. This atmosphere of accountability among a small group of Christian believers is nonexistent in the traditional congregation.

What is needed today is for a large body of laypersons to take the initiative in developing support groups whose concern is ethics. For reasons given in earlier chapters, it is very unlikly that such groups will be formed through the initiatives of the clergy. Some of us can indeed develop a ministry of organizing occupational groups whose chief objective is to raise up the ethical issues of a profession or institution in the light of Christian teachings. The organizers of such groups do need certain skills in small-group techniques, but there are many sources for help including a number of good books on the subject. But what is needed also is a recognition on the part of the church that there is a valid type of lay ministry in organizing and participating in a support group. Some linkage with the church should be established so that the lay developer-enabler can call in the necessary clerical support for theological input when needed, and so that the supportive imprint of the church is evident to all participants.

Laypeople are faced with sticky ethical decisions in every corner of their lives. Quite often these ethical decisions directly involve the welfare of other human beings. Is the church of Jesus Christ content with the way ethical decisions are being made in our society today? If not, it is not enough for our clergy simply to denounce the moral breakdown in society from their pulpits. It is not enough for national church bodies simply to issue position papers on major ethical problems of our time.

The way is clearly open to *do* something about ethics in our society. That doing involves the creation and support of thousands of lay support groups across our nation. Initiated by lay ministers who see this as their calling, and supported by a church organization that affirms its importance, a movement for creating lay support groups certainly has the potential for making a difference in the moral climate of our country.

8.

THE MINISTRY
OF THE
CHANGE AGENT

Both the Old and New Testaments make frequent reference to prophets and prophecy. An entire section of the Old Testament is categorized as the Books of the Prophets. In the New Testament prophecy is one of the gifts of the Holy Spirit which the apostle Paul describes in his letters to the Romans, Corinthians, and Ephesians.

Today we define *prophet* as one who can predict the future. In the biblical sense, a prophet was more than a forecaster. The prophet had the role of being a social critic and an advocate of change. Prophets in the Bible were those who would highlight the evils of the day, and call for repentance and a change of direction.

A contemporary word for *prophet* is *change agent*. In today's usage, the change agent is one who responds to an injustice in society by calling attention to it and by acting to try to correct it. It is in this sense that I understand Paul to be saying that some of us are called to be prophets and that prophecy is a gift of the Spirit. If Paul were writing to the church at Ephesus today, I feel he would say that some of us are called to be agents of change because we have been blessed with the talents and skills to help remove injustice in our society.

The ministry of the change agent—or the prophet—is an important and necessary ministry for some of our laypeople today. To illustrate some of the dimensions of such a ministry it is necessary to go back quite a few years, since change itself can only be seen in retrospect.

The civil rights movement of the early 1960s focused our family's attention on the matter of racial discrimination. Through the recommendation of our pastor, I became a member of the board of directors of a church-related community center in a black neighborhood of center-city Philadelphia. This association led to other types of involvement. Judy and I taught in a few black churches. Together with other members of our congregation, we began a sister-church relationship with a downtown black congregation which involved joint worship, picnics, and other social events. In short, we became rather closely involved with the urban black community and for a while it seemed to make sense.

The more time we spent with our black friends in Philadelphia, the more we became aware of the degree to which the white suburbanites were contributing to the problems of the center-city people. While many of us worked in the city, we lived in bedroom communities. We made little or no contributions to the city in terms of leadership, taxes, or political involvement. Indeed, the center-city people claimed that the suburban communities restricted blacks from securing housing outside the city limits, and thus prevented many from escaping the trap of the ghetto.

It was this charge of housing discrimination which particularly stung us. How could we possibly support the blacks in their struggle for civil rights in downtown Philadelphia if, in fact, our own communities were restricting their civil rights?

The Social Ministry Committee of our congregation met to discuss the issue of open housing. It was decided that we should first contact the realtors in our area to determine their policy. Without exception, every realtor assured us that they did not discriminate in any way for reasons of race, creed, or nationality. We were pleased.

Then the Johnsons arrived. Bob Johnson was a black man who had just been transferred into the Philadelphia area by a large nationwide concern for which he worked. He was a skilled professional, earning enough money to buy a home in almost any part of our metropolitan area. We came to meet him because he was also a member of our denomination, and one of his interests was to find a home reasonably close to a Lutheran church. Our suburban area was one of several he was considering because of the good school system it offered for his two children.

Since several of us had been in touch with the realtors just a short time earlier, we offered to show the Johnsons our community and put them in touch with some real estate agents who would help them out. It was then that our eyes were opened to the truth.

Without exception, each realtor had nothing to offer which would meet the needs of the Johnson family. The only available homes were either far above their price range, or so far below their minimum standards that they were totally unacceptable. It was devastating. I well remember going back to the office of one of the real estate agents I had interviewed a few weeks earlier and angrily charging that he had not been truthful with me on the matter of open housing.

"Mr. Diehl," he said, "I told you what I knew you wanted to hear. It was not a complete lie. I do support the principles of open housing. But I must make a living. If I begin even showing homes to a black family, my competition will let everyone know about it and no one will give me listings. I agree with your ideal, but I can't help you. When you get all the other realtors of this community to agree to show homes to blacks, I'll be happy to go along. I can't take that first step."

When we tried to bypass the realtors by ringing doorbells of homes which had For Sale signs out front, the word spread quickly. Our church office, pastors, and councilmen began receiving complaints that a few of us were out "block busting." It was startling how quickly reaction set in.

The Johnsons were not surprised; they were disappointed. Bob Johnson asked that we discontinue our efforts. He said he wanted to find a community where his family would be welcome.

Since his new assignment involved a fair amount of travel, he did not want to leave his family alone in an area that was hostile to them. As the Johnsons drove off, with those two lovely kids waving to us from the back seat of their car, we were ashamed and angry with our own community. The ugly truth had come home.

Several of the families in our church agreed that our area needed a fair housing organization to deal with the problem. Would this be part of the social ministry program of our congregation? Our church council said no. The issue was too hot, and a number of members did not agree that blacks had the right to buy homes anywhere they wanted to.

We soon discovered that there were other concerned people in other congregations who felt the need to start a fair housing organization. A planning meeting was held in our home, and in a few months the Upper Main Line Fair Housing Committee had its first public organizational meeting.

We were a diverse group. While we all shared the objective of open housing in our community, our philosophies differed. There were some who were experienced in social action and insisted that we begin by picketing realtors and engaging in straw buying. Those who were making their first venture into social action argued for educational programs. This group, and Judy and I were among them, wanted to hold public forums and offer speakers to church groups in the belief that people of goodwill would join us in a massive request to local realtors to make open housing a reality.

The beauty of the fair housing committee was that it took people where they were and permitted them to work in that direction which seemed most appropriate to them. The activists began picketing real estate agencies, and the community became angry. Those favoring education held open forums and the community was indifferent. The only ones who showed up were those already committed to the cause. Few churches showed any interest in our speakers' bureau.

As picketing continued, reaction began to develop. The local clergymen, all of whom supported our cause, got complaints in increasing number and intensity from their parishioners. Some of the most outspoken opponents of fair housing also happened to be some of the wealthiest families in the churches. The clergy quickly got caught in the middle.

I was a member of our church council at the time, and frequently there were heated debates over the matter of open housing. Although our pastor was a member of the fair housing committee, he also had the responsibility of keeping our congregation from splitting up over an issue. At the time I was bitterly disappointed about the lack of depth of his commitment to fair housing, but now I understand the role-identity problem with which he struggled.

I had to assess my own role when, after one heated church council discussion, the group voted that I could not link my activities in the fair housing field in any way with my role as a member of that church council. I debated resigning from the church council but our fair housing group felt that I could do more by staying and continuing to confront others with the issue of discrimination. We began to receive a bit of hate mail, and one family in our church even went so far as to complain to the management of my company about what I was doing.

It became obvious that the advocates of education were getting nowhere. Those who picketed were getting newspaper attention, but there was no evidence of the realtors changing their viewpoints. As Judy and I were reviewing the ineffectiveness of our efforts, we were confronted ourselves with the issue of straw buying.

Straw buying is a technique used to prove that someone has illegally engaged in discrimination. It works this way: If a black family is interested in a particular house or apartment advertised in the paper, but they have reason to believe there may be discrimination in the area, they secure the help of two white couples. The first white couple visits the house or apartment to determine if it is available. As soon as they leave, the black family makes its visit. If they are interested and decide to take the property and the seller agrees, there is no problem. But if they are told that the property is no longer available, or has just been rented or sold, a second white couple appears as soon as the blacks leave. If the property is once again available, the couple puts down a deposit to hold the real estate and immediately reports the matter to the State Human Relations Commission or whoever is responsible for enforcing nondiscrimination laws.

The activists of our fair housing committee had been engaged in straw buying for a number of months, and had been responsible for bringing into court several landlords who were violating the law with respect to rentals. The effectiveness of the activists was dwindling, however, as more of the real estate people began to recognize them. What was needed was some new faces for straw buying.

Our committee discussed the ethics. Some felt that since it was impossible to engage in straw buying without telling lies, they could not do it. The activists argued that there was no other way to prove violation of the law, and that the greater cause justified the lies. Neither group tried to make the other feel guilty, but quite obviously it was a case of situation ethics.

Judy and I thought about it for many days before we decided. A week later we were out on our first straw buying assignment.

If telling lies in the cause of justice is an evil, like most evils it becomes easier to live with the more frequently one does it. The change agent therefore must always be reviewing the morality of his tactics.

The approach which turned out to be most successful was our boycott-reward program. Prospective sellers and buyers were asked not to do business with real estate people who practiced housing discrimination. Whenever there was evidence of a realtor offering housing in a truly open manner, his name was freely circulated in our newsletters. A significant turning point was reached when one of the largest realtors in the area began advising his clients that he was obliged by law to show his real estate to all interested parties and, if they did not agree, he could not handle their business. Although some of the more cynical members of our committee were not convinced, we decided to reward the announcement by strongly encouraging sellers to list their homes with this agent. Soon other real estate agents announced the same policy. The logjam had been broken.

When, a year later, we too moved, I made it a point to turn over our home to the agent who made the first move. I told him why we were doing it.

"Mr. Diehl," he said, "I do appreciate what you have just told me. But I appreciate more the fact that you and some others forced me to do what I knew was right all along."

I am not so naive as to believe that all housing discrimination has been erased on the Upper Main Line. It has not. And I am aware that the most effective means of discrimination in housing still exists—poor blacks from our urban ghettos can't afford to buy expensive suburban homes. But there has been a change. And I am convinced that today a Bob Johnson could buy a home in that area with little or no opposition from the real estate agents.

This is not a spectacular story. It was repeated in thousands of residential areas all across our nation in the 1960s. But it is useful in illustrating some basic principles and characteristics of a ministry of the change agent.

First, the change agent is not out for purposeless change. He or she focuses on a specific issue. For the Christian change agent the issue must be related to the faith. Our involvement in fair housing sprang from our conviction that discrimination is inconsistent with the teachings and lifestyle of Jesus Christ.

Change agent ministries may involve causes which are either ad hoc or continuing. The open housing effort can come to an end if discrimination in housing is eliminated. On the other hand, change agents can become involved in an ongoing ministry which works for justice in a community. Judy and I have been associated with the Allentown Committee for Equality for a number of years. This group acts as an advocate for those powerless people in our community who have been treated unjustly. As such, the group's attention may shift from housing to education, to prison reform, to health care, or to whatever other issue needs our attention. But the focus at any moment is always on a specific issue.

A second general point which the fair housing story illustrates is that change agent ministries must have support groups. Change almost always is resisted. Resistance brings tension and controversy. Most of us cannot function in controversial issues without some support group to back us up. When our church would not support our efforts at fair housing, we moved outside of it and formed our own new support group.

Another point to note is that we started where people were. Not everyone agreed upon the tactics. Activists were ready to hit the streets. Those of us who had never been on picket lines before opted for educational programs. Similarly, the lay minister change agent starts where he is and grows with events and experience. The entry requirement for a ministry of the change agent is not that one be a radical, but that one be willing to commit his Christian convictions to some form of action.

However, idealism in itself is not enough. Our fourth observation is that skills are urgently needed if change is actually to be effected. An experienced change agent could have saved our fair housing committee a great deal of wasted time and energy.

For example, a fundamental rule of institutional change is that people normally respond out of self-interest. Our public forums were largely ignored; they posed no threat to the community. Picketing of real estate agents got public reaction because it didn't seem proper in our genteel community. But it didn't threaten the realtors. Straw buying was very effective in the rental field because people began to get hauled into court over violations of the law. The boycott-reward program turned out to be effective because one real estate firm saw a way to turn it into its own best self-interest. The point is that ministries in institutional change require some degree of training in order to be effective.

A fifth point is this: Each change agent must carefully review his own ethical position as he tries new tactics. I place high value on the truth, but I lied in behalf of fair housing. I strongly favor orderly change, but I have taken to the streets to support mass demonstrations. I believe in obeying the law of our land, but I temporarily redirected—to President Nixon—certain federal excise taxes on my telephone bills as a protest against the war in Vietnam. In each case the situation called me to respond in what for me was an unethical way. I hope, pray, and believe that my actions were in keeping with God's will in my life. The important thing is to make certain that we always recognize that these decisions are exceptions to our ethical code, not changes in it.

Finally, the fair housing story illustrates that if the change agent is on target with his issue, there will be no "winners" and "losers" when the change is effected. All of society should be winners. The real estate agent who thanked me for helping to push him into change was sincere. Ultimately, all of society must benefit from the change.

For those who would consider a ministry as a change agent, I recommend two books which have been of great help for me: *The Change Agent* by Lyle Schaller and *Rules for Radicals* by Saul Alinksy. These two books do an excellent job of describing the nature of change, the style of change agents, and techniques for effecting change.

If conservative, middle-class, churchgoing people concede any validity at all to the ministry of the change agent, it is almsot always considered to be an activity for the young, or the poor, or the minorities, or the political revolutionaries. We have only recently emerged from a time when the term "hippie" was commonly applied to any person or group advocating social change. Generally we assume that our change agents will be those whose interests are at odds with the establishment rather than those who are comfortably situated within it. It is vitally important that the modern prophets, or change agents, include a generous number of conservative, establishment people.

Although we commonly assume that the Old Testament prophets were the outcasts or "hippies" of their day, a more careful review of the facts will indicate otherwise. Many of the famous Jewish prophets were conservative members of their religious establishment who heard God's call to speak out against the injustices committed against others.

The anti-Vietnam War protests of the 1960s were largely initiated by the youth who, quite obviously, had a large personal investment in the unfolding events. The decision makers in our government at first ignored and then tried to suppress the growing peace movement. For years the protests had little or no observable effect on the conduct of the war itself. Then came the Kent State killings. We and a lot of other older, middle-class conservatives were forced to take a much closer look at what was going on in our country. Although our family had not agreed with the United States policy in South Vietnam, it wasn't until Kent State that we concluded that the peace movement needed the active support of more than the youth. And as the peace demonstrations across the land began to swell with middle-aged, middle-class change agents, more of the leaders in Washington began to change positions.

Very few of my business associates became active in the peace movement. I joined the Business Executives Move For Vietnam Peace, but could find no one else in our city who was willing to become a member. However, the fact that I, a basically conservative, middle-class, middle-aged, middle-management business executive was marching with the peace groups in Washington forced many of my associates to take a serious look at the issues involved. Over a period of time, positions began to change.

So it is important that we have conservatives as change agents, too, and if that sounds like a contradiction in terms, it is simply one more of the seemingly paradoxical elements of the Christian faith. Certainly the makeup and direction of any movement for social change should be largely controlled by those whose interests are most directly involved. People must assert freedom; it cannot be given to them by others. But movements which arise out of the injustices of our society deserve the attention and support of all.

A group which had been deeply involved in a rather structured way in the ministry of the laity as change agents was the Metropolitan Associates of Philadelphia. MAP pointed out that people are affected by the institutional structures of society in two ways: they are workers within the institutions, and they are part of the general society which is affected by their practices. Whenever the actions of the institutions humiliate, enslave, and decrease options for people, there must be efforts to change them.

Although most attempts to change the institutions of society have come by way of outside groups putting pressure on institutional leadership, MAP advocated a supplemental action whereby laypeople were equipped to work for change inside the institutions in which they participate as employees or members. This proposition offers lay ministry possibilities for thousands of laypeople. It points to an entirely new direction for church support of lay ministries.

Robert A. Gallagher, a member of the staff of MAP, writes, "The church will need to think in terms of a lay ministry system which can help the change agent develop a critical awareness of current institutional incoherence, long-term commitment, long-range planning skills, a vision of new possibilities, authority reference points, a belief that problems are solvable challenges, an open view of the future, and a support community." The philosophy and experimentation undertaken by MAP provides both interesting reading and a guide for significant ministry of laypeople as change agents.

Our institutions of society can change for the benefit of people as a result of efforts directed both from within and without those institutions. But either way, it is obvious that potential exists for many Christian laypersons to connect their faith and life through identification of and support in ministries of the change agent—our modern prophet.

9.

EQUIPPING CENTERS
OUTSIDE THE
CHURCH

Two of the conclusions to come out of the 1974 consultation of the World Council of Churches' Department of the Laity are important enough to repeat. First, the laity must be agents of their own formation. Second, there should be more development of unofficial Christian communities apart from the ecclesiastical structure.

These two findings represent sharp departures from the efforts at lay renewal in many American denominations over the past twenty-five years. They suggest that instead of lay programs being designed by the professionals operating out of denominational headquarters, the initiatives have to be taken by the laity itself. And instead of trying to channel all lay ministry programs through the ecclesiastical structures of our churches, encouragement should be given to the development of unofficial Christian communities and groupings where the laypeople are.

Mark Gibbs and Ralph Morton wrote: "If the local church is not equipping its members for the life of the world, then there will have to be a revolution in the life of the local church as well as in the total structure of the church. Whatever happens, some form of local groupings will emerge for the self-education of Christians in their immediate situation." In recent years a form of local grouping *has* emerged. We call it the "house church" and it is almost universally a lay-initiated phenomenon.

About five years ago we were entertaining three other couples for dinner in our home. The conversation began to center on our various experiences within the institutional church. Two of the families had ceased their association with the church; two other families were actively involved. All of us shared similar feelings of a lack of depth existing in the religious groups with which we had been associated. We traded "war stories" and it seemed like each one added a new indictment against organized religion. Finally, someone asked the question, "What would it be like to live as a Christian in society today if, by magic, the institutional church suddenly vanished completely?"

We began to speculate. We saw Christianity centering in the homes. We saw small Christian communities developing. We pondered the styles of Christian education for our children. The possibilities seemed to excite everyone. Soon we were talking about the possibility of an "experimental Christian community." Before the evening was over we had agreed to invite some others into an experiment in Christian living in which the institutional church played no role whatsoever. The experiment proved to be so successful that the group has continued as a house church ever since. For those not familiar with how a house church operates, it is necessary to provide a bit more detail.

The name of our house church is FOCUS, an acronym for Families Of Christians, Uniting, Supporting. It consists of thirteen families of twenty-three adults and twenty children. Six of the families are active members in traditional church parishes representing three denominations. Seven of the families formerly were active in the church but dropped out due to the failure of their congregations to provide the type of support they felt was necessary in relating faith to life today. It was to the FOCUS Community that Nancy Smith and her family came when they felt it necessary to leave their church. There are two former clergymen in the Community, but their role is the same as that of any other member of the group. In areas of biblical knowledge they do have more expertise, but then our scientist members have greater skills in their respective fields also. Those families which are still associated with the institutional church all agree that FOCUS has provided their lives with a dimension of Christian community which they have been unable to find in their traditional congregations.

The general operational style of FOCUS has changed very little during the past five years. Every other Sunday morning the total Community gathers at the faculty house of a local college for breakfast and a worship-study period. Families take turns providing the simple breakfast and leading the morning program.

The worship experience is designed by the parents and children of the family having the responsibility for that day. The styles of worship vary from traditional to contemporary. At times we have included group dance in our worship. Prayer is usually open and spontaneous from the group. FOCUS worship is a clear departure from the traditional church services in which the liturgy has been designed by unseen and unknown professionals for consumption by their clientele, the laity. Worship in the FOCUS Community is relevant to the real-life experiences of the group and springs from the innermost thoughts and concerns of all its members.

The educational period, which is woven into or follows the worship experience, is also designed by the same parents and children. Generally, a theme has been established by the Community to extend over several sessions. For example, over a period of several months we studied various families in the Bible, with each of us selecting a favorite Bible family and presenting a learning session on it. Frequently the educational periods involve such things as role-playing, small group discussion, skits, and use of visual aids. Efforts are made for the study periods to have an experiential dimension to them—hence such things as role-play.

Because of the great range of age among our children (from three years to the late teens) the educational programs for FOCUS present quite a challenge. While these learning periods may lack the comprehensive content of institutionally designed curriculum materials, they far exceed parish religious education experiences in freshness, excitement, and total involvement of people. When children and parents together plan an educational program, or when they participate in one planned by their friends, our young people clearly see that this matter of the faith is important to their parents. Contrast this approach in Christian education to that of the institutional church where parents drop their children off at the doors of graded classrooms, never to be involved in or even to witness the exploration of the faith. I believe the example we set before our children as we struggle to learn about our faith and to share it with the rest of the Community is a far more enduring type of learning than that which most children get in their Sunday church schools.

On alternate Sunday evenings, the adult members of FOCUS gather in a home for discussion, study, sharing of life experiences, and providing of mutual support. At times the group may review a religious book or essay. Sometimes there will be a series of evenings devoted to study of topics of current interest—the juvenile justice system, the charismatic movement, an investigation of prayer. The style of our evenings together is such that the agenda can readily be switched to that which is needed by one of the members. A member of the Community is thus free to bring up anything that is happening in his or her life which he or she would like to share with friends. It may be something to celebrate; it may be a pressing problem. The group does not demand more of a person than he or she is comfortable in revealing. Thus members are able to share some of their deepest personal problems with the Community, knowing they will be treated with respect and tender concern. Others may prefer to reveal less of their personal life to the group; they are not on that account made to feel guilty.

Over a period of years there have developed mini-relationships among the larger group of thirteen families. A family which may be reluctant to share a deep personal problem with all the other twelve families may feel very comfortable in sharing that same problem with one or possibly two of the families. Under such circumstances, confidentiality has been very well maintained.

Not only are individuals able to share their concerns with the rest of the group, they can rely on support from the other members. If one of the members is performing in a concert somewhere, the rest of the group will show up. If a member runs for a political office, the group actively helps in the campaign. When a new baby is baptized in a church, the group comes and sits together as an extended family. Thus the sharing of family problems, of job concerns, of town and neighborhood service efforts, or of other personal experiences provides effective support and love for the individual members unlike anything I have ever experienced in a traditional congregation.

About once a month, the entire FOCUS Community schedules a social event. Adults and children, functioning as a large extended family, may have a picnic together, charter a bus to New York, go square dancing or bowling, take a hike or camp out overnight, or attend a cultural event. On some Sundays we may forego our usual program and instead visit a local church to participate in its worship and study program. These visitations have involved many different denominations.

Twice a year the community has a weekend retreat at Kirkridge in the Pocono Mountains of Pennsylvania. Again, the entire program of study, worship, recreation, and personal growth is designed and presented by various families in the group. Generally the retreats have been milestones in the growth and development of the Community.

At times the FOCUS Community will undertake a project unrelated to the needs and interests of the members themselves. For example, when General Amin expelled the Indian families from Uganda, we offered to become sponsors for a large Ugandan refugee family. We rented a place for the family to stay, rounded up furniture, clothing, and food. Several members of FOCUS went to New York to meet the plane from the refugee camp, and escorted them back to our town. We helped the Ugandans find jobs and become settled in their new land. Although the children could speak English, we had to get the mother and grandmother to English classes. Over the past three years our relationship with the Ugandan family has continued in a supportive role. We attend their weddings and funerals. We offer help when problems arise for them. The experience has helped to broaden all of us, but our children have seemed to benefit the most from it as they have witnessed their parents working at expressing the Christian faith in active works of love.

The FOCUS Community maintains a communal treasury. Various families contribute to the treasury as they are able. Whenever the group has an event which costs money, such as a trip to New York or a weekend retreat, the necessary money is taken from the treasury. In this way, no family is restricted from participating in an event because of the cost involved. When the treasury is low on funds, an announcement is made and within a period of weeks there is money enough to do whatever needs to be done.

FOCUS has become an extended family. It is not at all uncommon to see the children of one family eating a picnic lunch with the parents of another family. For those of us with teenaged children who are in the process of breaking ties with home, the relationships they have with other adults we admire and love is a source of comfort during trying times. We have come to recognize our limitations as an extended family, however. We witnessed the breakup of one of our early member-families. While we tried to be helpful, we found the husband and wife were both turning to us for personal support which would be used against the other. We were caught in the middle. When the divorce finally came, many of us felt a deep sense of the failure of our Community. Since then we have come to recognize that our relationship as an extended family cannot solve all the problems of the members, any more than a natural family can. But in spite of failures, the positive side of having such an extended family relationship is overwhelming.

Clearly, FOCUS has provided all of us with a style of Christian life and support which has been absent in the traditional parish structure of the mainline denominations. Lay-initiated and lay-designed, this house church has been for us a bridge which links faith to daily life.

FOCUS is not unique. There are thousands of house churches all over the country.

They have come into existence because of a failure of the traditional church structure to provide real support for its individual members. And, it is important to note, virtually all of the house churches have been initiated by the laity.

No one person set out to design or promote the house church movement. It is a phenomenon of our times. It developed almost spontaneously across the nation. And, of greatest significance, it represents what is necessary to meet the needs of many dedicated Christian laypeople at this time.

Some house churches are more intense than others in that they involve communal living. Some are less formal. While house churches vary in form and style and program, and no two are alike, there are several elements which are common to all.

First and foremost is the element of support. Every successful house church has a style and atmosphere in which each member feels he truly has the support of the others. He is known and accepted where he is by the entire group. His joys are celebrated, his talents affirmed, his efforts supported, his failures shared, his doubts understood, and his growth nurtured. This type of support can only occur if the group is small enough to enable members to get to know each other in depth.

Size, then, is a second common element of all successful house churches. Either the group itself is small or it has carefully structured itself into intentional small groups so that in-depth relationships can be developed. There is a sense in which the individual is accountable to the group and the group is account-able to the individual.

Finally, the focus of the house church is on meeting the needs of the people. Its form and program are flexible. Too often large congregations consider how the members can serve the institution. The house church considers how the institution can serve the members.

Laypeople can form a wide variety of equipping centers outside the structure of the church. Judy is in a neighborhood prayer group which meets every Tuesday morning. There must be thousands of people in similar ecumenical groups, but how many more could be developed? The Detroit building contractors met as an occupational group. In how many other cities could occupational and professional groups meet regularly to try to relate faith to work? In the research department of my company an ecumenical group meets once a week at lunch time for Bible study. In how many other organizations could clusters of employees meet to relate their faith to work? The National Yokefellow Prison Ministry brings Christians together to work with the inmates of federal prisons. In how many communities and in how many ways could Christians gather together to share a common ministry to the poor, the handicapped, the sick, the elderly, the estranged? Our Upper Main Line Fair Housing Committee brought the people of God together in a common ministry for a cause. In how many other causes can Christians group together as a response to their faith—hunger, world peace, refugee resettlement, governmental reform, equal opportunity?

Not only are there countless possibilities for lay groups, there are also sufficient models and resources already in existence to help new ministries to form. For example, the Faith at Work organization of Columbia, Maryland, with its magazine, newsletters, conferences, training programs, and consulting services, can provide excellent assistance to lay groups seeking to get started.

It is unfortunate that many people who are already engaged in vital lay ministries are among those who say they are unable to connect their Sunday world to their weekday world. The fault, of course, lies in the fact that the religious insitution is incapable of recognizing and affirming lay ministries beyond its own walls.

The churches *must* do something about that fact.

10.

SUPPORT
FROM THE
CHURCH

Bob Miller was perhaps the best Scoutmaster I have ever known. He loved boys and they loved him. His effectiveness in teaching, leading, and providing a good example for his Scouts was outstanding. He spent much of his spare time with the boys, individually and collectively. But he carried a small burden of guilt all the time we knew him.

Bob was constantly being asked by various members of our congregation to serve on a committee, teach Sunday School, usher in church, or perform some other service in our parish. Because of his total commitment to the Scouting program he always had to say no. And every time he did he felt guilty about it.

Some of us tried to tell Bob that the service he was performing so well as a Scoutmaster was a more important Christian contribution than being an usher in church. He never quite believed it, because his church never proclaimed that fact.

The first thing the church must do to develop and support lay ministries is to proclaim in fact what it preaches in theory. We are all called to ministry in life. We have different gifts and can serve in different functions. The coming together of Christians in a congregational relationship is not an end in itself. It is a means to an end. We come together for worship, education, the Word, the sacraments, and fellowship *so that* we can be effective agents for Christ in society.

The church needs to breathe life into the doctrine of a universal ministry. It can do this by active involvement in three areas: interpreting, affirming, and equipping. Interpreting the concept of lay ministry takes place at a number of levels of the organized church. The traditional method of interpreting a doctrine at the parish level is through the sermon. Many clergy have preached on the subject, and they should continue to do so. But rather than continue to deal with generalities, sermons should offer specific models of what a ministry of the laity is really like. This can be done by citing examples of ministries in life as well as by asking laypersons to share some of their own efforts at ministry through occasional sermons presented by them.

In a similar manner, the parish newsletter should have articles about and by members of the congregation who are developing their own particular styles of ministry. In both sermon and newsletter care must be taken not to concentrate only on the "successful" reports. Perhaps one of the most important realities about the ministry is the many failures which are encountered. As we struggle and experience failure, it is important to know that others share our disappointments. Moreover, care must be taken that the citing of examples does not develop an elitist group within the congregation, nor convey the impression that salvation is gained through good works. Honest, simple expressions of witness are needed.

Some congregations try to emphasize the need to scatter the faithful into the world through the use of symbolic elements in their worship. Instead of snuffing out the candles after the conclusion of a service, some congregations have the lighted candles lead the processional out of the worship area. The symbolism, of course, is that the light is to go out into the world. Some parish bulletins conclude the order of service with the printed words, "The worship is ended; let the service begin." Similarly, some church buildings have appropriate signs posted about exit doors for all to see as they leave: "Go and do likewise," "Go you, therefore," and "You shall be my witnesses" emphasize the mandates of Jesus to all of us.

Regional, district and national offices of the various denominations can interpret the doctrine of lay ministry through their communication channels. Newsletters, magazines, television, and radio can be used to explain and particularly to illustrate it with a liberal use of specific examples.

As long as we speak of a doctrine of a universal ministry, care should be taken that the official documents of the church be more specific in their language. One national denomination defines its membership in terms of "congregations and ministers," while they really mean "congregations and *ordained* ministers." The general term *minister* should be used when reference is made to all the believers, lay and clergy alike. The term which defines function within the church structure should more precisely be *clergy, ordained ministers,* or *pastors.*

Once the concept of a universal ministry has been established and its interpretation begun it is necessary to have continued *affirmation* of the reality of the doctrine. This affirming can occur in a variety of ways.

Every time I have been elected to the governing body of my congregation there has been a service of installation. All the newly elected members stand up in front of the congregation. The duties of our office are read to us. We are usually asked to state that we will endeavor to fulfill those duties to the best of our ability. The congregation in turn is often asked to pledge its support to the new leaders. And finally there is a prayer offered in behalf of our service to the parish. In a similar manner I have been involved in congregational affirmation of my service as a Sunday School teacher and a Scout leader. Judy has been involved in comparable choir recognition services. A healthy congregation has many ways of affirming the work of laypersons as they serve the parish.

Have you ever seen a congregation affirm the work of laypersons as they serve the world? I have not. Suppose on a given Sunday the worship were to be built around the ministry of physicians, or schoolteachers, or housewives? Suppose at some point members of the profession selected for that day stood in front of the congregation while the pastor briefly described the scope of their ministries. Suppose the congregation was asked to support them as best they could and prayers were offered for those ministers. I should think such services would be mighty affirmations of the ministry of the laity.

One can usually determine the priorities of an organization by looking at its budget. Local parishes must affirm their support of lay ministries by budgeting for training and support programs.

Clusters of parishes or church districts can affirm lay ministries by planning special services for occupational groups. May 1 is considered "Law Day" throughout the legal profession. On a denominational or ecumenical basis a group of parishes could very well plan a worship experience in which the emphasis would be to relate law and justice to our religious roots. Why should the celebration of Law Day be exclusively a secular event? In similar manner, other occupational groups could on occasion be brought together for worship, and to search for their ties to the faith.

At the national level, denominational news releases, church magazines, and other communication channels can affirm the universal ministry by the selection of the materials they will use. National conventions of the various denominations should provide opportunities for affirming lay ministries. Programs should allow time and space for lay groups to meet and interact. If there are display areas which feature the "work of the church" they had also better deal with how the church supports the ministries of its members in society.

Besides interpretation and affirmation, lay ministry needs undergirding at the point of actually equipping the lay ministers. It is in this area of *equipping* that the church organization can provide the greatest support.

Just as worship can serve to interpret and affirm the universal ministry, worship must also be seen as a focal point for spiritually equipping laypersons. The sending out of the believers must be more than an intellectual thing; it must be a spiritual event. Laypersons must be able to feel a part of that flow of power which comes from God and then goes out into the world through them.

I know Christians who believe that all things are possible if we trust in God enough. They then play down any suggestion that we can learn to be more effective instruments of God's will by improving our skills. I do not believe the good Lord gave us a brain so that we could ignore it. When Jesus first sent out his Apostles, he instructed them to "be as wise as serpents and as innocent as doves." That's pretty clear. And while I too believe that all things are possible if we trust in God, I'm equally convinced that he expects me to use my talents in the best way I can. Therefore, education must be a cornerstone of the equipping for lay ministry.

Most congregations are already well structured for educational programs. That's good and bad. Good in the sense that education is recognized as a part of the program and budget of a parish. Bad in the sense that the stereotype so often is that education means Sunday School for little children. Education for lay ministry must be different enough from what has been for so many years that there can be no doubt about its intention.

I recently led an adult group in our parish through a course in lay ministry. We met in a tiny classroom during the regular Sunday School period. Because the walls were thin, the noise level from children's classes on either side was distracting. It was not conducive to good study. But the worst feature was that most of the core of our congregational leadership was unable to participate in the course because they themselves were teaching classes. A number of people told me they wished so much that they could participate in the study, but they had to follow through on their responsibility to teach, and rightly so. Equipping laypersons for ministry is a serious business. It deserves special attention in the parish, and should not be just another offering in the church school program.

Some of the content for equipping has already been mentioned in previous chapters. All of us should have a course on effective listening. For those who see themselves in a ministry of the "aid man," courses in first aid, psychology, sociology, counseling, and interpersonal relationships might make sense. For those whose gifts lead them toward verbal communication of the faith, courses in Bible, theology, and communication skills seem indicated. For those whose ministries carry them into ethical struggles which affect the lives of others, courses in ethics, economics, logic, and decision making come to mind. For those who move toward being the change agents of society it would be well to be skilled in organizational dynamics, psychology, communication, and governmental studies. Because the range of ministries is broad, the skills required are obviously diverse.

Since most learning comes from doing, the closer we can reproduce the doing the better we can learn. I am a great advocate of role-playing in a classroom setting. Initially it is sometimes difficult to get people to play roles in front of others. Once the ice is broken and a trust level develops, most people enter into the learning experience with vigor.

Since all of us, at one time or another, will interact with another person in connection with the death of a loved one, Christians should have some skills in relating to others at the time of death. A series of role-plays is an excellent basis for developing those skills which work best for us. For example, the group leader might read the following scenario:

"You have just discovered that your next-door neighbor's seventeen-year-old daughter has been killed in an automobile accident. You have never talked to him about religion. You feel you want to help him in some way. You go next door. What do you say?"

Two volunteers then play the roles as naturally as they possibly can while the rest of the group observes. After a period of time the role-play is stopped and discussion begins. Possibly another person or two may wish to make a try. The discussion opens up all kinds of comments and sharing experiences; frequently people relate actual experiences they have had or tell of one they are presently struggling with. A number of different scenarios involving death can be worked up, each of them providing the group with new insights into theology, psychology, and communication skills.

Role-play as a learning technique dovetails perfectly with the basic premise about lay initiative in lay ministries. The laity design the scenarios, act out the roles, comment on the events, and relate everything to actual experience in their lives. The role of the clergy is one of listening and of interpreting the situation theologically. The whole experience is rooted in lay initiative with professional support from the clergy.

One of the more effective ways of equipping the laity is through weekend retreats. The days a group spends together at a conference center provide for a concentrated learning experience free from the distractions of normal family responsibilities. Where children must be cared for, a simple technique is to share the baby-sitting. One group will go on retreat while the second group takes the children of the first group into their homes. Then at some later time, the second group leaves while the first group tends the children. Expenses should be borne, at least in part, by the congregational education budget for lay ministries.

Education is a continuing thing. It is unrealistic to expect that a parish can schedule good educational events which, when completed, will assure a continuing lay ministry. One of the most essential elements of a ministry of the laity is that there be well-defined support groups. The weekend retreat can sometimes lead to the formation of such support groups on a continuing basis.

The house church is probably one of the most common and effective support groups of our day. It functions well to assist individual members in their joys and sorrows, successes and failures, certainties and doubts. We have discovered that, given the right circumstances, a house church can also operate success-fully *within* a congregational structure.

After we had been involved with the FOCUS Community for several years I began to speculate whether a somewhat similar type of house church community could function well within a parish. Together with another FOCUS family who happened to be members of our congregation, we put together a slide show of the FOCUS Community to present to our church council. We asked that we be given permission to have a one-year experiment to see what would happen if such a group functioned under the umbrella of our congregation. While the pastor liked the idea, the council was unimpressed. The decision to let us proceed for a year was arrived at after we pointed out that it would cost the congregation no money—a classic example of a right decision being made for the wrong reason.

Through letters and bulletins we advertised the experiment widely so that everyone who had an interest knew they were welcome to join us. We started out with about the right number—eight families numbering twenty-five people.

Following somewhat the same form as FOCUS, we decided to meet as total families for worship, study, and a meal every other Sunday evening. On alternate Friday evenings the adults only would meet in homes for study, discussion, and support. We were very careful to set up our program in such a way that it would not compete with events in the larger congregation.

We called ourselves "Channel 2." The name expressed a certain self-understanding. Just as the various channels on a television set provide alternative programs, Channel 2 provided another style of Christian relationships within our larger fellowship. It was meant not to compete with the program of the congregation but to supplement it.

Channel 2 became an immediate success, and with it came some problems. For one thing our family-style educational programs became so stimulating for our children that they began to balk at going to church school. They argued that they got more out of Channel 2, and they were right.

The problem of exclusivity also cropped up. Despite the fact that we constantly were inviting others to join the group, we began to hear complaints that we were too exclusive. The fact was that we began to find such a supportive relationship with each other that we tended to do many things together. We found a type of Christian fellowship and love which was impossible to reproduce in a larger congregation of people. The pastor saw this and supported us as he tried to explain to others that what they saw as exclusiveness was really a close Christian caring relationship among a group of people.

Channel 2 had several retreat weekends which were milestones in the deepening of the group. We had a number of purely social events which also brought us closer together. When problems arose, when there were joys or sorrows, the Channel 2 Community was always there to provide support.

After the first year had elapsed, we were given official permission to continue, although some efforts were made to turn us into a service organization for the congregation. It took constant interpreting to remind our congregational leaders that Channel 2 did not exist to serve the congregation; it existed to support its members as they tried to relate faith to life.

When our pastor left a few years later, and our family moved, Channel 2 ceased to be an element in the life of that congregation. However, years later, the remaining members of Channel 2 still got together in our homes to renew the fellowship we had found and treasured. We can still count on each other for support.

In our present congregation we belong to a small support group which meets in the homes every other Friday evening. This group is not a fully developed house church since we seldom involve our children in our get-togethers. We meet to study about the faith, pray together, and share each other's concerns. We are accountable to each other in our efforts to link faith and life. The relationship of Christian support continues to grow.

There are congregations in which support groups can flourish and are encouraged by the clergy. There are congregations where support groups are seen as threats to the clergy and are stifled. But support groups are so essential to lay ministries that if they cannot exist within a congregation, laypeople must form them outside the parish.

One of the overlooked facts of life is that perhaps no one needs a support group more than pastors themselves. The image that we impose upon our clergy today makes for a very lonely life. We continue to expect them to be absolutely unshakable in their convictions, totally removed from sin or error, aloof from the economic pressures of life, and the head of an ideal family with no problems. No human can fill that bill. But to whom can our pastors turn in their failures to measure up to that standard? How can they truly get support if they are unable to reveal their problems?

We have had clergy in almost all of our small groups. Some parish pastors are able to open up and share. Others have been too afraid to risk. If there is no willingness to be vulnerable, there can be no support. Yet it is equally true that when the pastor finds a support group within his own congregation, there are complaints from others that he is playing favorites. I have also observed clergy meeting with each other in occupational types of support groups. More often than not such groups are characterized by competitiveness, defensiveness, and no real honest caring. There are no easy answers. As laypeople seek to minister to each other through support groups, they must not overlook one of their number who is in vital need of support—their parish pastor.

Equipping of the laity can occur through the efforts of clusters of churches or district groupings. With the support of a larger number of congregations, special "theme" conferences can be held to which prominent laypersons or theologians can be invited. The range of themes is as broad as the issues which confront the laity every day of their lives. Business ethics, abortion, prison reform, ecology, and many other topics presented by experts in the field can help the laity relate faith to the issues of the day.

Congregations acting together can also organize occupational support groups. With such groups case studies are useful for delving into the ethics of real-life situations. A problem is given to the group in the form of a case study. Usually the problem is so complex that there are clearly no easy or "right" solutions. The group tries to establish values and test them against Christian teachings. Again it is helpful if a theologian can sit in as an observer and interpreter. Time and time again I have found that we will conclude with that blessed assurance that in a world of imperfect solutions we are acceptable to God solely on the basis of our faith in him. That message cannot be repeated too often.

District church groupings can sponsor such equipping aids as lay institutes at local colleges and lay schools of theology at seminaries. It is at this level that leadership for lay ministry support groups is developed. Leaders are trained in theology, group dynamics, and leadership skills. Leadership retreats are regularly scheduled to provide a continuing development program for lay ministry facilitators.

At the national level there should be sponsorship of events which facilitate lay ministries in key areas of decision making in our country. Is it possible that under the sponsorship of national church bodies, and upon the invitation of prominent lay members of these churches, there could be faith-life dialogues among key members of government, industry, education, the communications field, and the military? Here again, prominent theologians would be present, not to be judgmental, but to listen and ask the questions related to the faith? Some efforts already have been made along these lines but they are still far too few.

Finally, national church bodies can support the lay ministry movement by establishing a climate which permits lay initiatives to develop freely within and between the various denominations. This can be done in several ways.

First, the organizational structure of the denomination should be flexible enough to permit varieties of Christian communities to exist. The tremendous popularity and success of the small-group movement suggests that there could be important benefits to be gained if there were multiple forms of Christian communities in addition to the traditional parish. In his book *The Base Church* Charles M. Olsen describes a wide range of possibilities for Christian community in which the form of structure is the result of the needs of the group.

Second, it is time that the professionals in our national denominations offices begin spending less time tinkering with the *forms* of worship and begin dealing more with the *nature* of worship. When surveys continually reveal that laypeople find great difficulty relating the Sunday worship experience to the weekday life, perhaps the liturgical elitists in our denominations had better start listening to the laity talk about their struggles in that weekday life. Gibbs and Morton say it well: "Worship still seems to depend on the work of scholars; it still needs to be explained by the clergy. Worship thus becomes something at second hand for the laity." An action which has to be explained to people quite obviously does not arise out of their daily lives. "Worship is something a man does, not something he watches someone else do."

In a similar manner, the Christian education materials being turned out by our national denominations are too often designed by scholars far removed from the arenas of life where laypeople try to bring—and live out—their faith. Church school books continue to provide answers for questions no one is asking. It is highly important that educational materials be the result of a serious—and successful—listening to laypeople if they are to be useful in meeting needs. It may be too early to judge whether the educational methods employed by the house church have been more successful than the traditional Sunday School, but there is reason to believe that they have. It would be well, therefore, for our church educators to encourage the laity to experiment more with different means for self-education at the local level.

Despite indications that the organized church exercises less and less influence in our society, laypeople still have a significant degree of respect for their national church bodies. It is not easy to take initiatives which may run contrary to the patterns of an institution you respect. Therefore it is highly important that our national church leaders work to create a climate in which lay initiatives can develop.

"The time has come to make the ministry of the laity explicit, visible, and active in the world. The real battles of the faith today are being fought in factories, shops, offices and farms, in political parties and government agencies, in countless homes, in the press, radio and television, in the relationship of nations."

Those are good words and true. They come from a report on the laity issued by the World Council of Churches. The only problem is that the report is dated 1954. More than two decades later there is still no indication that the WCC has met with any success in making the ministry of the laity "explicit, visible, and active in the world."

By 1974 that same World Council had come to the conclusion that "the laity must be agents of their own formation." The shift in focus is crucial. What is being said is that our church bodies have come to recognize that they cannot "make" the ministry of the laity.

If the gap between Sunday faith and weekday world is to be closed, if the gap between what the church proclaims about a universal ministry and what it does about this doctrine is to be closed, it will be because of initiatives taken by the laity. And that is the calling for faithful men and women today who will no longer tolerate any separation between their Christianity and real life.

NOTES

page

1   "Eli M. Black": See Mary Bralove, "Giving Up" and "Power Struggle," *The Wall Street Journal,* 7 May 1975.

12   Hans-Ruedi Weber, *Salty Christians* (New York: Seabury Press, 1963).

12   Frederick K. Wentz, *The Layman's Role Today* (Nashville: Abingdon Press, 1963), p. 39.

18-20   Listening-to-Lay People Project: See the Report of the National Committee of the Listening-to-Lay People Project, adopted 2 November 1970, presented to the General Board of the National Council of Churches, 23-27 January 1971, especially pp. i, 3-5, 14.

20   "Consulting Committee on Affirmations of Faith": See William H. Lazareth and Raymond Tiemeyer, *In, Not Of* (Philadelphia: Lutheran Church Press, 1974), pp. 86-87.

25   Elizabeth O'Connor, *Eighth Day of Creation: Gifts and Creativity* (Waco, Tex.: Word Books, 1971).

25-26   "Luther": See Gustaf Wingren, *Luther on Vocation* (Philadelphia: Fortress Press, 1957), p. 72.

26   Hans-Ruedi Weber, *Salty Christians*; Hendrik Kraemer, *Theology of the Laity* (Philadelphia: Westminster Press, 1958); Mark Gibbs and T. Ralph Morton, *God's Frozen People* (Philadelphia: Westminster Press, 1964); Mark Gibbs and T. Ralph Morton, *God's Lively People* (Philadelphia: Westminster Press, 1970).

page

26   Peter L. Berger, *The Noise of Solemn Assemblies* (Garden City: Doubleday & Co., 1961), p. 167.

26-27   John A.T. Robinson, *Honest to God* (Philadelphia: Westminster Press, 1963), p. 134.

27   Colin Morris, *Include Me Out* (Nashville: Abingdon Press, 1968), p. 19.

28   Gibbs and Morton, *God's Lively People*, p. 195.

31   Pierre Berton, *The Comfortable Pew* (Philadelphia: J. B. Lippincott Company, 1965), p. 68.

32   Gibbs and Morton, *God's Frozen People,* pp. 22-23.

34   Berger, *Solemn Assemblies,* p. 37.

39   "The 1965 Consultation": Resolution adopted by Plenary Session of an ecumenical consultation organized by the World Council of Churches' Department on the Laity and the Permanent Committee for International Congresses of the Lay Apostolate (Rome), Gazzada, Italy, 7-10 September 1965.

40   Frank W. Klos, "Report on the Ecumenical Consultation, New Trends in Laity Formation, Assisi (Italy), Sept. 7-17, 1974."

46   "PACE": See William E. Hoffman, "Employees' Personal Problems Called Widespread Factor, *American Metal Market*, 30 May 1975.

68   Robinson, *Honest to God*; Joseph Fletcher, *Situation Ethics* (Philadelphia: Westminster Press, 1966); Harvey Cox, *Secular City* (New York: Macmillan Co., 1965); Jürgen Moltmann, *Theology of Hope* (New York: Harper & Row, 1967).

69   Thomas A. Harris, *I'm OK, You're OK* (New York: Harper & Row, 1967).

70   D. Elton Trueblood, *The New Man for Our Time* (New York: Harper & Row, 1970), p. 117.

page

70-71   Wallace E. Fisher, *Can Man Hope to be Human?* (Nash-
         ville: Abingdon Press, 1971), p. 141.

79   *On-the-Job-Ethics,* ed. Cameron P. Hall (New York:
         National Council of the Churches of Christ, 1963).

81-82   "Robert C. Batchelder": ibid., pp. 38-41.

93   Lyle E. Schaller, *The Change Agent* (Nashville: Abing-
         don Press, 1972); Saul D. Alinsky, *Rules for Radicals*
         (New York: Random House, 1971).

95-96   Robert A. Gallagher, "Ministry of the Laity as Agents of
         Institutional Change," *NAES Journal,* April 1972.

97   Gibbs and Morton, *God's Lively People,* p. 129.

104   National Yokefellow Prison Ministry, Inc., Shamokin
         Dam, Pennsylvania.

104   Faith at Work, Inc., 11065 Little Patuxent Parkway,
         Columbia, Maryland.

116   Charles M. Olsen, *The Base Church* (Atlanta: Forum
         House, 1973).

116   Gibbs and Morton, *God's Lively People,* p. 69.

117   "Make the ministry of the laity explicit": *Evanston
         Speaks,* (Geneva: World Council of Churches, 1955) p.
         64.